earth
angel

Earth Angel

THE AMAZING TRUE STORY OF A YOUNG PSYCHIC

Ross Bartlett

 A GODSFIELD BOOK

Dedication

I dedicate this book to two people.

Firstly, to my Nain – a lady who always believed in me and to whom the word 'special' doesn't do justice.

Secondly, to my grandfather – a man who has played an enormous part in my life.

Contents

Great Spirit, Infinite Consciousness, please hear me and please help me. My guides and helpers, spirit friends, please hear me, please help me. Please help me link up as strongly as possible to you in the spirit world. Help me to make as great a connection and communication to the spirit world as possible. Help guide me during this demonstration. I ask that the messages people receive are the ones that need to be given. Please help me to give readings that focus on evidence and proof of survival, of names, road names, full addresses, personality descriptions, descriptions of physical body, conditions of passing, feelings, emotions and memory links. Please help me for the good of the people, to show them love and to awaken them from a spiritual slumber.

Introduction

I'm a medium, and I can't think of any other job in which your personal performance is scrutinized quite so minutely. People judge you on your accuracy, how direct you are and how evidential – that's the phrase I use to describe information of a very specific nature, relevant to the person for whom I'm 'reading'. This is what my clients want when they approach a medium. A medium can't rehearse beforehand – I address the public directly and I'm completely on the spot. So, why do I put myself in this position? What is it about the work that keeps me doing it, day in, day out?

I've always tried to be the best medium I can be because I want to help people. It's as simple as that. When I start a reading I like to go in straight away with a contact's first name or, if not, the reason they passed when they did and the circumstances around it. I roll on from there: I describe their personality, then add the name of the road they lived on and the number on their front door.

Details like those, straight from the spirit world, make the experience of mediumship real and emotional for so many people – they sit up and take notice. As I build the evidential links during a reading, my client's expectations rise – the higher you raise the bar, the more he or she expects. And however well I do in one reading, my client expects me to be as good or even better next time.

People come to spiritualist churches for my public demonstrations and book me for private readings when they want to ease their grief after the passing of a loved one and find greater clarity in their lives. Often emotions are running high. At such a time people need accuracy, and it's my job to give it to them. I never forget that.

I readily admit that my age and the tattoos on my arms and neck (I also have one on my back, but you can't see it!) make me stand out from the crowd. When I walk onto a stage I must seem a little different from most mediums. Many are aged between forty and sixty. As I write, I'm twenty, and have been giving readings since I was fourteen. I turned professional when I left school at sixteen and, as far as I'm aware, I'm one of the youngest professional mediums in the world.

At a time when most teenagers are thinking about going to university, how to get hold of the latest video game or where they'll go on their next big night out, I was thrust into a world of spiritualist churches, private readings, amazing trips abroad and voyages of learning that took me (and still take me) from the disciplines of spiritualism to Native American culture and a belief in different levels of energy.

Even though I'm only twenty, I've achieved, seen and heard so much in such a short space of time that

I've hardly had time to take stock of the experiences that have shaped me. I'm writing this book because I'd like to share with you some of those experiences and try to explain how so many different cultures and areas of knowledge are relevant to the way we think. I've been lucky: I've met so many amazing people and have been involved in situations that would make your hair stand on end. At the end of the day, though, I'm still just twenty.

And this (in mediumship at least) sets me apart. As do my tattoos. I have lots, on both arms, my neck and my back. I love them, and each one is important to me in a different way. Up and down my right arm I have stars and sparkles, which represent our connection to the sky and the universe. This was my first tattoo and symbolizes my belief that the physical and the spirit world are connected. We're at one with the universe and the universe is at one with us. We're a living, breathing part of it and its energy, as is the spirit world. We co-exist with it throughout our physical lives.

The Eye of Horus appears on the left side of my neck. It's a symbol from Ancient Egypt, meaning vision, wisdom and protection, and reflects my love of ancient cultures. It reminds me that we can all be wise, protective and spiritual people. Just above the Horus you'll find a pentacle, a Pagan symbol that represents the universal circle, another reminder that we're all made from the energies and elements that exist in the universe.

The Ankh, also a hieroglyph from Ancient Egypt, is tattooed on the right side of my neck, signifying eternal life, and below that is the Om, used in Buddhism and Hinduism: it refers to the vibration of universal creative consciousness. Some people call this God, but for me it has more to do with the pure energy and consciousness we're all part of.

Vines and Yiddish words snake up the length of my left arm. The words are incredibly personal to me, and act as a daily reminder of who I am and why I do what I do. Forgive me if I don't translate them for you, but they are my own private message to myself.

Last, I have a huge tattoo of an angel's wings on my back. I don't see myself as an angel but, like an angel, I'm a messenger put here for one reason: to help, guide and heal people by connecting them to the spirit world. I'm a conduit, a link between the physical and spirit worlds, which are always connected, living side by side and influencing each other. An Earth Angel, if you will.

I understand that my age and tattoos attract extra attention when I visit a spiritualist church for a demonstration. But I never worry about what people may think of me, because when I'm onstage my mind is tuned in to do the best job I can. That's why I say the prayer you read at the beginning before every demonstration and reading. It helps me to connect in the best possible way to the spirit world, to open the channels as wide as they can go so that I can give the best possible readings.

Ritual is important to me and my work. It starts when I get up. I say a prayer, especially if I'm demonstrating that day. As I say it, I think about that day's readings, and send out thoughts to help with them. I'll ask for help from my spirit guides, my ancestors and the Great Spirit or Universal Consciousness.

I'll also make 'prayer ties': square pieces of cotton fabric that I fill with tobacco leaf. We all know what tobacco has become in Western society but Native Americans consider it a sacred herb. When I make my ties I send out prayers and intentions in the belief that what I put out there, I'll get back. That's one of my key beliefs. It's at the core of my meditations: what you put out into the universe, you will get back. I wear my prayer ties around my neck when I do a demonstration.

Once I get to a spiritualist church, I find a quiet place – it might be a room behind the stage. There, I'll say some more prayers and meditate to get my mind into that special place, and to make a good strong connection to the spirit world.

Then, and only then, I'm ready to face the audience. The audience who expect so much from me, and have seen me develop from a nervous teenager into a young man who is completely at one and connected with the spirit world, the Great Spirit and divine consciousness. The patterns and symbols on my arms, neck and back give me focus, empathy and love for the individuals in the crowd.

Standing on that stage, I'm ready: I'm in the zone and feel fully connected to the spirit world.

It's time to get to work.

I need to be able to access that zone quickly, whatever the situation and wherever I appear. Recently I was asked to do an interview for a community radio station. I'm always more than happy to share my knowledge, especially with those who are cynical about mediumship, and because I enjoy media work and believe that I should be as open as possible about my calling, I had no qualms about doing the interview. To me, the spirit world should be available to everyone so that they can benefit from it.

At the station's headquarters I met the DJ, Imran, who was going to interview me. He wanted a bit of a chat before we went on air. When he'd first contacted me, he'd also asked if I could do a reading for him, perhaps because he wanted to check me out and see for himself what I was about.

'Very nice to meet you, Ross,' he said, smiling and shaking my hand in the reception area. 'I've heard some of your other radio interviews and read some magazine articles about you and I must say I'm very impressed. You know, even some of the places that are usually very negative about your sort of work only had positive things to say about you.'

As opening lines go, that wasn't bad, especially from someone who wanted a reading before he talked to me on his radio show. Maybe Imran wasn't as cynical as I'd thought he would be. In fact he was very friendly, and as he led me into his office he told me more about why he wanted me on his show.

'I've seen a lot of mediums in the media, but your age makes you stand out, makes you more interesting. You're a lot different from what I imagined.'

I hear that often, and if my age and tattoos make me stand out there's not a lot I can do about it. But it can be an advantage not to fit the stereotype. If my youth and appearance make people want to talk to me, give me an opportunity to help them understand the spirit world, put them in touch with special people who have passed over and open their minds a little, I'm fine with it.

When we got into his office Imran became a little more guarded. He explained that, although he had been born into Islam, he had no strong religious or spiritual leanings and certainly didn't believe in an afterlife. He was due to interview me on air shortly, and I realized I was about to undergo a sort of test – if I impressed him the interview would go well.

We sat down, and immediately he moved his chair in front of mine to sit as close to me as he could without feeling uncomfortable. Some people think that the closer they are to me, the harder I'll find it to deduce things from their body language. I once saw a sceptic do that with a medium on TV: he said he wanted to be as close to the medium as possible so that the medium couldn't tell if he was fidgeting or betraying emotion when he asked him a question.

Imran was the same. His rigid sitting position and expressionless face told me he was going to try to make the reading as difficult for me as he could.

Many sceptics don't understand that body language or position doesn't matter during a reading. It has no effect on how clearly I can contact the spirit world. Mediumship is not about reading someone's mind or looking for clues in a raised eyebrow or a slight upturn of the lips, or even how someone answers a question. It has nothing to do with any of those things. It's about the spirits coming through, my connection to them and, of course, what they're saying in relation to the person sitting in front of me. That's how mediums can give readings remotely, or use psychometry (touching an object owned by a particular person and divining information about them through the item) to good effect.

Sceptics think that mediumship is reliant on carefully placed, leading questions, body language and a subject's answers. If you ask enough of the right kind of questions, you get the right kind of answers. That's the theory, but it isn't the way I work. That's why I like to start any reading with evidential information: it dispels the notion that I must be getting it from the sitter, and it proves I don't work from body language or facial expression. Imran was trying his best not to give anything away.

Almost as soon as we were both comfortable I was immediately aware of three people coming through to talk to him. People often ask how I make contact with people who have passed. Is it a feeling? An image? A sound? An emotion? The best way I can describe it is like this: when you're in a crowd – maybe at a station or an airport – and you're waiting for someone you know to emerge from the exit, your eyes move around, looking for that person to appear. When you spot them, the rest of the crowd sort of melts away. It's exactly like that: a pull to a particular person.

When I'm doing a public demonstration with lots of people in one room and I'm confident that my connection to the spirit world is solid, I become aware of spirits stepping forward and making themselves known to me, helping to guide me to a particular person in the crowd. Once I'm connected to a spirit, I'm suddenly linked to their thoughts and can recognize when they're focused on someone. I feel what they feel; I see what they see; I hear what they hear. I'm at one with the spirit.

It's different when I'm doing a reading for one person because there isn't a crowd to wade through, but the concept is almost the same – I feel or see someone step forward in my mind, plug into what they're feeling and convey what they want to say.

In that instance it was just me and Imran, sitting facing each other. A spirit makes himself or herself known in various ways. Sometimes it's with a feeling, at others I might hear a voice or even see the spirit in my mind. That's when I can start to ask them questions and get answers that only the sitter will know about.

That was what it was like with Imran. It's interesting when you read for someone from a traditionally non-British culture because the customs are different and perhaps memories are slightly different from what I'm used to. The spirits may convey images and details that are different culturally. And let's not forget language. They may not have spoken English while they were here in physical form, so the names are very different-sounding and sometimes they can be hard to hear clearly. Sometimes my mind, which always wants to make sense of anything it hears or sees, even changes them to something I understand better in my language – a name from a different culture might change to Harold, for instance, even though it's not Harold at all, just the closest thing my mind can grasp.

But these three people were coming through clearly. There were two men and a woman. I was aware that one man was coming through more strongly than the others. Thanks to feelings and images he was showing me, I also became aware that he seemed to have had problems with breathing and digesting. As the contact continued it became evident that he had had cancer, which had spread throughout his body. Even so, the images and feelings he was showing me made him sound like a strong, stern character. I relayed all this to Imran and he nodded silently.

That's the way I like to conduct readings. However painful or joyous the information that comes through from the spirits I contact, I always put forward the evidential information to everyone for whom I give readings. It helps to break the ice and the subject sees straight away that there is more to mediumship than they'd thought.

Despite the initial hit, Imran was still in stoic mode.

'The gentleman says he was really frustrated at not being able to get up and move around during his final months, and that during the last two weeks of his time here he deteriorated very quickly,' I told him.

'Yes,' Imran said.

'He's telling me about his home, and that it was in the country away from the city. He's saying that you and your family would visit him there.'

'Yes,' he said again, accompanied by the merest suggestion of a nod.

'The gentleman is showing me he had a moustache. And he's telling me about a black-and-white photograph in the family, a photograph of his immediate family.'

'Correct.'

There was a pause. I've done enough readings to know that Imran's current demeanour couldn't last for ever, and there would come a time when he would show me how he was feeling. Information about family members who have passed can melt the stoniest exteriors.

'Yes, correct,' he said again. 'It sounds just like my uncle. He died of cancer and those last two weeks were a really horrible time for my family.'

Imran was beginning to engage in the reading, and as I continued he lost his poker face. I could see that he was shocked. Here was a man who had no spiritual or religious beliefs, yet I was bombarding him with information that only the man with whom I was in contact, Imran and his family could know about.

'The gentleman is bringing forward a lady,' I continued, 'and she wants to be acknowledged in a motherly fashion. But I get this feeling with her. This feeling of impact. That's the only way I can describe it. Impact. Like she said she was hit by something ...'

'Yes.' Imran nodded. His shoulders – which had been so proud and straight only minutes before – had hunched, and his face seemed pleading. His eyes were misted with emotion. 'My mother ... She died after being hit by a car.'

The bond between mother and son is very strong, and many of my clients become emotional when their mother comes through. This woman was showing herself to be very kind and caring. She had dedicated her life to helping others, and it was little wonder that the thought of her was tugging at Imran's heartstrings.

And it wasn't just Imran with whom this contact was resonating: his mother was shedding a tear or two at being able to communicate with her son. Even spirits can be overwhelmed at being in contact with a loved one from the other side. From their perspective, the 'other side' is the physical world that we live in.

'She's giving me a name … the name Hussain? And she's asking if she can bring forward another gentleman with the name Hussain. He's saying that he passed because of a heart-attack, but the name Hussain had been passed down through the family. The uncle carried this name too. Can you understand the name Hussain, Imran?'

'Yes! Yes, I can,' he said enthusiastically. 'Hussain is my family name, and my middle name.'

'OK, good. That makes perfect sense,' I replied. 'The gentleman is now showing me a link with the armed forces. Definitely the armed forces. He's letting me know how proud he was of what he achieved when he was in this world. I get this feeling of strength, of real masculinity, with him.'

'Yes … This is really ringing a bell. Can you tell me what else he's saying?'

'He's giving me more names … Hassan, Fatma, Hamza, Nadia and the Islamic version of Mary …'

'Yes!' Imran smiled, relaxing back into his chair. 'I have relatives with those names.'

I paused to receive the next piece of the puzzle, trying to let the feelings and images settle in my head before I could relay them.

'The gentleman is showing himself in my mind going up to you and giving you a clip around the ear.'

Imran laughed.

'He's saying that whenever he wanted to get your attention or tease you when you were a little boy he'd go up behind you and give you a playful clip, and have a few words with you in a humorous way.'

Imran nodded, still smiling and totally relaxed now.

'He's saying that even though he'd give you a clip, he'd always kiss your cheek afterwards.'

'You're right,' Imran said, shaking his head. 'He really did do that. It was all part of the banter. Our relationship was quite a playful one, but he was always very loving. I can't believe it. Here I am, a man who doesn't believe in the afterlife, communicating to three deceased family members!'

He couldn't believe the amount of detail he had just heard from three of the most important people in his life, all of them in the spirit world. The uncle who had died from cancer, his caring mother who had passed because of a motor accident, and the man who would give him a playful clip, followed by a kiss. This is the type of relationship any man would recognize, the type of activity that stays with someone for the rest of their lives, becomes a cherished memory and is passed down through the generations.

That last man was Imran's father.

Psychic Awakening

I was five when I had my first contact
with a person in spirit. I remember it so well; it almost
feels like yesterday.

Most five-year-old boys are tearing about the
house, playing with their toys and existing in a happy,
innocent world of their own. My world comprised
my grandparents and my mum. We all lived in the
same house, and were busy doing our usual things:
my grandfather watching his beloved football, my
grandmother – I called her 'Nain', pronounced 'nine',
the Welsh for 'Nan' – cooking, cleaning or reading
her magazines, and my mum out working. This was
the world I knew. There had been no real shocks or
surprises or any strange occurrence in my family home;
no uninvited guests, nothing out of place. At least until
that one evening.

I was lying on the bed in my mum's room, with
its pink wallpaper, huge wardrobes and portable TV
perched on the bedside table. There's something about
your parents' bed when you're a child – it's so vast and

comfortable that you can't resist rolling around on it, stretching out and not being able to touch the edges with your arms or legs. It feels huge. Lying on my mum's bed made me feel closer to her and the adult world.

I switched on the TV. There were only four channels on that portable set – BBC 1, BBC 2, ITV and Channel 4. Changing channels, pushing buttons. Bored, bored, bored. I decided to go downstairs and see what my grandfather was doing. I switched off the TV, headed towards the door and turned off the light.

As I was walking through the doorway I stopped. Something was wrong. Or different.

In the twilight I saw that, behind me, the TV was still on, its fluorescent glare illuminating the room.

That's funny, I thought. I know I turned it off. I scrunched up my face, puzzled. Like most children of that age, I didn't think about the whys and wherefores. I'd simply switch it off again. Push more buttons. And if it didn't work, I'd move on to something else. But as I turned back into the room and approached the TV, I realized it wasn't showing the channel I had been watching when I'd turned it off. It was hissing – an eerie noise – and blurred black-and-white lines were running across the screen, the picture you get when you haven't selected a channel.

This was odd: if I hadn't turned it off, surely it would still be on the channel I'd been watching. I stared at it for a few moments, as it hummed in its own hypnotic way, then reached out a hand to turn it off again. I pushed the button and the noise stopped.

The TV's gone wrong. Time to go downstairs and see my granddad.

I turned away from the TV and saw a woman standing at the end of the bed, looking at me. Not in a quizzical way, or a threatening way, not even in a happy way. She was simply looking at me with a neutral expression. Now, at that stage in my life I knew only a few women – my mum and my grandmother being the main ones – and this one, standing at the end of my mum's bed, was neither of them. There was something about her I couldn't place, and a sense that she didn't belong washed over me. Not just in our house, but in that period of time. She didn't wear the same sort of clothes as my mum wore, or any of the women I saw hurrying along the street. Her hair was different too.

I'd watched enough television to know how people dressed. The white dress that woman was wearing seemed old-fashioned, with buttons right to the neckline. Her light brown hair was tied neatly in a little bun, and she had a round, kind face. She looked older than my mum but younger than my grandmother, and I noticed a pretty black brooch pinned to the left side of her dress.

I had no idea how she had appeared or what and who she was. When you're five you can't explain something like that. I could've told you about characters on TV and my mum or grandmother. Pretty. Ugly. Tall. Short. Long dress, short dress. Happy face, sad face.

Yet this woman was not a ghost, or not as I imagined a ghost might look like. This person from the spirit world – for I know now that this was what she was – appeared to me like a real person, with a solid form that eclipsed the wardrobe behind her. I could not see through her. Thanks to TV and the movies, we think of ghosts as shimmery, almost transparent figures. This woman was as solid as solid could be.

And I wasn't frightened. Transfixed, I just stared at her staring at me. We didn't speak, just gazed at each other for what seemed like half an hour, but in reality was probably about ten seconds. I remember being intrigued and open. At that age our fears can be difficult to put into words. But I wasn't afraid: I hadn't been conditioned to fear interaction with anyone unfamiliar, including a person who had passed over. I experienced that woman as a real person, and she certainly didn't feel like a threatening presence. In fact, there was a real sense of calm in the atmosphere, and a sense of … I couldn't put my finger on it at the time, but now I can identify it as compassion and love.

Just as I was getting used to the spirit-visitor beside my mum's bed, she started to fade. There was a black coat hanging on the wardrobe behind her, and it became more and more visible. As she grew transparent, the coat and the wardrobe came more into focus until, finally, she was gone.

Naturally I was full of childish curiosity, and as soon as she had disappeared, I bounded downstairs with a spring in my step. Nain was reading a newspaper, so I snuck in next to her.

'There was a lady in Mum's bedroom.'

'Are you sure, love? Mum's not in. It couldn't have been her.'

'No, it wasn't Mum. There was a lady standing at the end of the bed. She looked nice.'

'Oh, that's good. If she looked nice there's probably nothing to worry about.' My grandmother was reassuring and matter-of-fact.

At that age I wasn't full of deep, meaningful questions. I didn't try to analyse the situation, just accepted it for what it was: a woman had appeared in my mum's bedroom and Nain had said there was nothing to worry about.

'Okay,' I said, as young children do when they switch from one subject to the next. 'I'll go and watch the football.'

'Good boy.' She smiled.

And that was what I did.

Now, I know what you're thinking. You're wondering why I wasn't full of questions, why I didn't want to understand what had just happened. All I can say is that if that experience happened to me now, without everything that had taken place subsequently in my life, I would've been full of questions. My grandmother wouldn't have been able to get a word in edgeways.

But I was five and had no words to express what I had seen except in the simplest terms. I do remember thinking, as I sat with my grandfather watching the football match, that the person who had shown herself to me wasn't a normal woman. But that was fine. Not normal was okay with me, especially if she was as kind as she looked. Now I know from her dress that she was possibly Victorian – maybe she had even lived in our house: it had been built in that era.

I thought about it some more. Where could she have come from? I didn't think she could have just walked through the big door downstairs. What about a window? No, it was dark and I knew Nain shut all the windows when it was dark. So, where could she have come from?

At that age I had a very basic understanding that a person who had died went to Heaven. I'd got that from my Nain, who was very spiritual. Like most children of that age, I didn't really understand the concept of dying. A relative might be there one minute and gone the next. If I asked where Nain's father was, she told me he was in Heaven with the angels. That's what parents and grandparents tell us. Could that woman beside mum's bed have come from Heaven? If she hadn't come through the big door downstairs or the windows, she might have come from Heaven. It wasn't something I knew for sure, but I had a strong feeling that that was where she had come from. I was comfortable with that explanation. It felt right.

What I didn't know was that this was to be the first of several contacts with the spirit world throughout the coming years. I was a normal child doing normal things in a stable and happy home, but things were beginning to change in other parts of my life.

Throughout my childhood I kept the memory of the spirit-visitor at the end of Mum's bed stored at the back of my mind, but it had no more significance to me than a sticker I received on my fourth birthday. I went to nursery that day and the staff laid on some little cakes and party hats, as they did for each of the children on their birthdays.

Aside from the cakes, hats and singing 'Happy Birthday', they gave me a sticker to celebrate my special day. It had a big number four on it, and a picture of a giraffe. But there was something about that sticker, something that made me smile and feel that I was king of the world. I stuck it on the headboard of my bed, where it stayed until I was eleven. It's funny how when you're a kid even the smallest things can seem the biggest and best in the world. And everything is relative – the sticker was just as memorable to me as my sighting of the spirit at the end of Mum's bed.

Living
with Spirits

I was born Ross William Bartlett, at
eleven twenty-five p.m. on 31 May 1992, in Southampton
– a city on England's south coast with a proud maritime
history. It is famous for its docks and the departure of two
of the most famous ships in global history, the *Mayflower*
and the *Titanic*. I first opened my blue eyes at the Princess
Anne Hospital.

My grandparents were at the very heart of my family,
particularly as my parents separated soon after I was
born. Of course I wasn't old enough to understand the
significance of this development – I was just living in my
grandparents' house in Wilton Road. My mum doesn't
talk about the past much, but it must have been hard for
her when my dad left: she went out to work to provide for
me. This wasn't unusual then and it isn't now, I know.
Many parents – both single and those still together –
go out to work at unsociable hours to make sure there's
money coming in.

Around this time I think one of Mum's jobs was
driving a forklift truck. Not many women did that

kind of thing back then (and they may still not!), and it shows what young parents have to sacrifice to make ends meet. During this time Mum did various different jobs, sometimes night shifts, and it was down to my grandparents to look after me when she wasn't around. I shared a bedroom with my grandmother for nine years and we were kindred spirits in many ways. Yes, I loved my mum dearly and I'm full of admiration for the way she went out at all hours to earn a living, but Nain was another constant in my life. We had a special bond, and she was my guardian angel. She was very open, which taught me from a young age to be open to everything.

Evenings were Nain's and my special time together. I'd climb into my bed and pull the duvet up to my neck, then look at my grandmother as she sat with me in the evening half-light. It was that magical time of the day when everything was warm and fuzzy, and Nain was at the heart of it all.

She'd tell me about her life as one of twelve children living with her family on a farm in Anglesey. Her simple stories mesmerized me: tales about animals and scrapes and how hard life was in the early part of the 20th century. Nain's stories always seemed magical, and I used to love conjuring up images of fields, valleys and farm animals as I was falling asleep. She would tell me how chickens pecked and jerked their heads back and forth as they walked across the farmyard; how she, with her brothers and sisters, would help geese and ducks find good places to lay their eggs; how giant pigs wallowed in squishy mud.

She liked to tell me about one goose that would attack the postman whenever he delivered letters to the farm. The thought of that bird waddling after the poor man and nipping his bum as he ran out of the yard made me giggle so much. It was a different world from the one I knew, but Nain made it vivid and real.

Visiting relatives in Anglesey when I was older, I could see why she loved to tell me stories about her childhood. I was always staggered by the scale and beauty of that part of Wales. There were fields as far as the eye could see, and after we'd been walking across them we'd go back to a great-aunt's house. There, with my coat still on, I was fascinated by her open fire. I used to sit for ages staring at the flames as the orange spears danced in the fireplace, and I could've listened to the crackle of wood for ever. I miss those days, and I know Nain did, too. Whenever we visited relatives she and her sisters used to sit together for hours on end, reminiscing about the old times.

Nain prayed every morning when she got up and again when she went to bed. But, unlike some people who are spiritual, she never tried to push her beliefs on anyone. She just put spirituality at the centre of her life and made sure that it informed everything she did. She believed that the spirit world was always close by and that people who had passed – especially those who were important to her – were close by, watching over us, and knew what was going on in our lives. She didn't talk about these things frequently, but the way she reacted to my spiritual experiences showed that she accepted there was communication between the two worlds.

So, even when I was very young, there was an atmosphere of spirituality in my house, a special undercurrent that had a subtle influence upon me, as if certain doors were being quietly opened. As I grew older and had my early spiritual encounters, quietly, slowly and surely, these doors were opened wider. I just had to walk through them.

I lived at my grandparents' house until I was about nine. They were great years for me; years I'll never forget. Not just because of the warmth and love my grandparents and mum showed me, but because my first spiritual experiences took place there. Those events unlocked something inside me, something I didn't understand at the time, but which grew as I got older.

Our modest house had a bus stop outside the front door. I remember hearing the buses rumbling up and down the street, then running up to the window and watching the passengers getting on and off, wondering where they had been and where they were going. This constant stream of buses and people meant it was a busy street, and inside the house it was busy too. I slept with Nain and Grandfather in one room while, to begin with, my mum and dad slept in the other. Five people in two rooms.

We also had five dogs and a cat. There was Ebony, a cross between a Great Dane and a German Shepherd, then Bryn, Karma, Sian, Muffin, and George the cat. I mention those animals because when I was nine Bryn played a part in one of my formative spiritual experiences.

It was late on a Friday night. Mum was out at work and my grandparents were upstairs in bed. There were perks to being left on your own at that time of the day. Every child dreams of staying up later than they should, and on nights when I didn't have to get up for school the next morning, Nain and my grandfather would let me stay up to watch TV or play video games until Mum came in.

In that respect I was a fairly free child and, within reason, I could pretty much do as I liked. But Mum and Nain worried about everybody and everything, a real pair of worriers. They were extremely protective, and I wasn't allowed to do things that some of the other kids did because they thought I might get hurt. So, there was no roaming about the neighbourhood at night, no running about in the streets or playing in the local parks unsupervised. But when I was within the safe confines of my house, I had a free rein.

That evening I was in the living room, and it was late. The American wrestling was on telly, and I loved it – I was in a world of my own watching those wrestlers crashing down on each other, so I didn't pay any attention when Bryn gave a low growl. He was lying between me and the glass door that separated the hallway from the living room. Eventually the growling became loud and clear. Maybe he had heard something outside or someone was stirring upstairs. He quietened for a while, but then began to growl again. This time it was no longer the low, slightly muffled reverberation you hear when a dog's lying on a carpeted floor. Bryn's growl was louder and he was projecting it away from the floor, into the air.

I looked around and saw that he was staring up at the glass door.

'Bryn, what is it?'

He sat up straight and went on growling at the door. I expected to hear people getting out of their car or perhaps a leaflet being pushed through the letterbox – that must have been what had set him off, surely – and fixed my eyes on the door.

On the other side of the glass door I saw a glow of white light.

'It's all right, Bryn, shush,' I said, patting his head as I edged slowly towards the door, wondering if my tired eyes were playing tricks on me. The nearer I got, the clearer the white light became. It was bright but fuzzy around the edges, with little discernible shape or form. It resembled a human hand.

I was moving towards the door and squinting to focus on the strange shape that was pulsating on the other side of the glass. The almost iridescent hand wasn't moving, but it wasn't connected to anything. It floated in the air as Bryn and I stared at it, shocked to the core.

Then, without warning, something banged on the door three times. BANG! BANG! BANG! I leapt towards it and flung it open, convinced those bangs had woken everyone in the house. I glanced up the stairs for any movement at the top. Nothing. The disembodied hand had gone. I looked down the hallway. Nothing. I looked halfway up the stairs. Nothing.

That violent noise couldn't have been caused by Nain or my grandfather moving about. The house was old and the stairs creaked – you could hear more or less every movement anyone made. Still, I ventured upstairs to check if they were awake. They were fast asleep.

I crept back downstairs. What had happened? It was all over so quickly. Thankfully, Bryn had calmed down and all was quiet, but I was frantically searching for an explanation of what had happened.

Even if Nain had walked past the door and got caught in the light, that wouldn't have explained the three bangs. And then there was Bryn – why would he have been growling at Nain? It was like he had seen something I couldn't see. I know now that animals can be highly sensitive to spirit presence, and this must have been the case.

For a nine-year-old who was revelling in being able to stay up late and was engrossed in the wrestling, this wasn't the kind of thing I had bargained on happening. Or not consciously. But several things had happened – and were happening – that made me question my place in the world and what was going on around me. Since I'd met the Victorian woman at the end of my mum's bed, I'd had other odd experiences, and they were starting to occur more frequently.

It turned out that our house had 'previous'.

Some years earlier, my mum and Nain had just come in after my great-grandmother's funeral. My mum, so the story goes, was upstairs and my grandparents were downstairs in the living room. They were settling back into their normal routine when the door — yes, the same door — started to shake violently. So violently that Nain and Grandfather looked up and my mum rushed downstairs to find out what was going on. The shaking lasted just a few seconds, but they say it was so violent it was unlike anything they had heard before. It made the whole house tremble and the door almost came off its hinges.

My grandfather — a highly rational man, army-trained — tried to find a reason for it, but the vibrations caused by a passing bus were no explanation: buses drove past the house at regular intervals every day and had never resulted in anything like that. And there had been no bus outside at the time. While the door was shaking, my grandparents and Mum said, it seemed almost to be vibrating from inside itself as if something was shaking it from the inside out.

Some years later, we discovered what lay behind the shaking door. My mum consulted a medium, who told her about the incident and revealed that it had been a visitation from my great-grandmother in spirit. Mum and Nain had just returned from saying goodbye to her at her funeral and she had evidently decided she would find her own way to communicate once more. The shaking door was her final farewell.

The Angel
and the Glass

As I was growing up, the instances of
spirit contact in our house became increasingly frequent.
One summer afternoon I witnessed another incident.

Hot and thirsty, I headed from the garden into the
kitchen for a cold drink. Nain was standing with her
back to me doing the washing-up. As I walked into the
kitchen I saw the familiar layout, with the kitchen units
stretching along one side of the room. I walked over to
where we kept the glasses to fetch one, fill it with squash
and gulp it down. I had a favourite glass. Isn't it funny that
most kids have a favourite glass or plate and won't eat or
drink something that isn't served in or on it? I was the
same. For me it was a Thomas the Tank Engine glass and
I was intent on using it for my drink.

A glass standing on the unit moved. It stopped me in
my tracks. I looked at Nain, but she still had her back to me,
busy with the washing-up and humming a tune. I turned
back to the unit. Had a glass really moved all by itself?

My hands were freezing cold as the glass continued
to move, slowly and very deliberately. It slid carefully

out of its place alongside the other glasses, and moved so far along the counter-top that it looked as though it might slide off the edge and onto the floor. But instead of crashing to the lino, it stopped at the edge and slid back along the unit. I knew that glasses didn't move on their own. They were there to be picked up, used, moved around by people. They definitely didn't do this!

This wasn't like a glass moving when it's just been washed. Then it's carried along by the water on its rim: this was something you might see performed by a stage magician, a real trick of the eye. Yet there was no way this could have been an illusion. I was watching a rogue glass with a mind of its own.

While I was trying to make sense of it, Nain had heard the soft scrape of glass on counter and had turned to find out what was going on. She had seen the glass's final stop-start-stop movements. We watched as it finally reached its destination, which was the microwave at the end of the unit. I looked at her. She looked at me. I wanted to ask her what on earth had been going on, but I couldn't speak. I wasn't sure what to do or say.

Nain, calm as ever, went to the glass, picked it up, put it back with the rest and returned to the washing-up. She glanced at me, saying something to herself in barely a whisper, as if she was acknowledging a spiritual presence. Maybe because she believed in an afterlife and the existence of the spirit, she wanted to give thanks that we had witnessed it.

'Nain, did you see that glass move?' I said excitedly, tugging at her apron.

'Yes, I did,' she replied.

'Why did it move?

'I don't know.' She smiled. 'Perhaps it wanted to go somewhere. Or maybe someone was moving it for us.'

'But who?'

'Well, we can't know that,' she said calmly, coming over to me. 'You know I told you about Heaven and the angels? Maybe it was an angel moving the glass.'

I looked at the glass, now safely in its original spot, then back at Nain. 'Was the angel thirsty, Nain?'

'Perhaps it was, Ross.' She laughed. 'Or perhaps it was just the angel's way of saying hello.'

'Is that how angels say hello?'.

'Sometimes, yes. Because we can't see them, they move things around to let us know they're here, looking after us.'

I was confused. Why would an angel move a glass to say hello? 'Why can't angels speak like we can, Nain?'

'So many questions,' she said, ruffling my hair. 'All we need to know is that angels are around us all the time. We may not see or hear them, but sometimes they let us know they're here by moving things. Now, how about that drink, eh?'

As she poured it for me, her calm soothed me. She didn't seem flustered or surprised, even though seeing a glass move along a kitchen counter of its own volition was out of the ordinary, to say the least. Even I was old enough to understand that. But it had happened: we had both seen it. And looking back, I think Nain, being the sensitive person she was, knew that this incident was of a spiritual nature.

Nothing else was said. As I gulped my drink from my Thomas the Tank Engine glass, I was still in shock, rooted to the spot. Nain was finishing the few items of washing-up, and when she had done the last plate she went up to the bathroom. When she left the room I walked over to the glasses and stared at them hard, willing them to move. No sign of a repeat performance. I picked up the glass that had moved, put it where it had stopped at the edge of the counter and left it there, staring at it. Nothing. It didn't move an inch. What I had just seen must have been some sort of trick, I thought. I checked the unit to see if it sloped. It didn't. The glass had slid to the edge of the unit, stopped, travelled back towards the microwave and stopped again. Glasses do not have built-in sat-nav systems, but it was almost as if it had known where to stop before it fell off the edge or bumped into something.

Could Nain have been right? Might angels have moved the glass along the kitchen counter? If they had, that meant they were all around us and I hadn't even known it. They must live in our house, too. Especially if they moved glasses in the kitchen.

I was still a child, yet the spiritual events I had witnessed in my grandparents' house were beginning to show me different ways of looking at the world: spirit people, light forms, Heaven, an angel and a moving glass ... I was becoming more aware of spirituality, and the more I thought about it, the more I began to get a sense of what death might really mean. This may sound unusual for one so young, but there comes a time for any child when the concept of death hits home.

Generally speaking, and unless anything terrible has already happened to a child, the bubble of innocence in which we all grow up rarely bursts. When someone dies, parents or grandparents will often tell children that the person who has passed has gone to Heaven or is now with the angels (as Nain did with me): it helps them to understand that their loved one has transferred from one place to another, and that they are safe; they still exist, but somewhere else.

I remember talking to Nain about a great-uncle who had passed. I didn't know him, but I was struggling to understand what death meant.

'Is he poorly?' I asked Nain.

'Not any more, Ross. He's gone to Heaven to be with the angels.'

'So, he's not here any more?'

'No, he's gone there,' Nain said pointing upwards, patiently. 'He's resting now. But he can see us and he's looking after us.'

'What's it like in Heaven, Nain?'

'Well, it's nice and safe. Somewhere safe.'

This concept is easy for a child to understand, but it doesn't tell the full story of physical death. Sometimes when a child grasps the true impact and significance of mortality he or she may be very upset. I remember a friend telling me that when he realized what death actually meant he ran upstairs to his mum, crying his eyes out and imploring her not to die. I guess this story isn't unusual, and the crushing moment when a child realizes that those close to him or her won't be around for ever comes to everyone.

But thanks to my spiritual experiences in Nain and Grandfather's house, which had made me think about 'what happens next', I was starting to feel that when someone dies, as we know it, perhaps it isn't the end. Maybe they stay around for ever in some form. This was an enormous concept for me to digest, and I was frustrated not to have all the answers. But the more I thought about it, the more convinced I became of some pretty startling conclusions.

I wonder how many children think about death. If you've experienced a bereavement in your immediate family you will have encountered it first-hand, but at that stage in my life I hadn't. Nevertheless I used to sit on the end of my bed thinking about death rather a lot, about what it meant, why it occurs and, of course, the sixty-four-million-dollar question: what happens after someone dies? I had thought a lot about my experiences with the Victorian spirit, the glowing hand at the door and the moving glass. I couldn't explain them in terms of the physical world, so I concluded that there was definitely something more. Something more. Something else. I hated not knowing what it was, but there was surely no other explanation for what I had witnessed.

Another thing I wasn't sure about at that point in my life was the concept of time and ageing. I was pretty convinced back then that I would stay young for ever. I never saw myself as an adult. I thought about Nain and my grandfather, my mum and dad. There was no way I'd get that old.

Of course time passed, but I was hardly conscious of it. I would get up, go to school and interact with my friends. I wondered how I could get to level fifty on my favourite video game, or what was on TV that night. It was a normal life for a young boy.

But then, out of nowhere, I began to hear voices. I would hear somebody calling my name in my head. I knew there was no ordinary explanation for these voices; I would hear them even when the house was empty, so they couldn't have come from a member of my family.

As well as this, I was having visions. The subconscious is an incredibly powerful part of the mind, capable of producing some amazing things, particularly during dreams when buried emotions often manifest as images. But my visions were slightly different.

They started when I was seven, and appeared either in daydreams or sleeping dreams. Nothing unusual there, but instead of random images and locations that morph into something and somewhere else, they would show a specific place and time. A few weeks after one of these experiences, I would find myself in the place and situation I had envisaged. In time, I came to accept that my visions were of actual events that were yet to happen.

For instance, in my grandparents' house there was a cupboard under the stairs and we used it for storage. In a vision, I saw myself in that cupboard while my mother was pulling things out of it. I was being shown an empty space inside it that she had already cleared. In the vision I wondered silently what she was doing.

A week later I got home from school to find my mum taking things out of that cupboard, apparently trying to find something. Bang! The sight in front of me corresponded exactly with what I had seen in my vision.

People often associate visions with bad things, like someone 'seeing' and predicting a plane or car crash. Back then my visions were confined to the world I knew. They wouldn't have made headlines, but they were the start of my spiritual development: I learnt to trust them and my intuition.

The visions have continued into my adult life. For the most part they predict normal events. Take my recent trip to Egypt. I'd had a vision a few weeks before – a daydream – about standing on a set of planks looking down on a particular group of rocks. I was on a cruise down the Nile. It was a real treat to see one of the world's great rivers in a country with so much history. I enjoyed seeing great monuments as the boat floated serenely along the waterway, but we also disembarked from time to time. On one occasion, I found myself walking across a set of planks to get off the boat. I was looking down so I didn't lose my balance, and in front of me was a rock formation that emerged from the water: the planks and rocks, at the angle I had seen in my daydream. I smiled to myself as I recognized what had happened.

During my childhood these glimpses of the future started to occur regularly, but always featured random, mundane events. I'd see a situation in my mind's eye and a few weeks later it would play out in front of me in the physical world. Most people experience déjà vu from time to time, but this was more than that, and the visions became part of my life; so much so that I didn't question them. I used to think they were quite cool – oh, look, here's another daydream; and, oh, look, here's what I saw in that daydream. With hindsight, I can see that this was part of my psyche opening up, my natural spiritual development. As the visions continued, I understood that I would always be able to see into the future. They weren't going away any time soon. That was for sure.

Nain's Vision

          'What do you want to be when you leave school, Ross?' Nain asked me one day.

'I don't know.' I shrugged. 'Why?'

'Haven't you thought about it at all? You're fourteen, you know, and it'll soon be time to leave school and start a career.'

'Well, there's a few things I've sort of thought about …' I was a bit pensive because I didn't like being put on the spot, especially about that sort of thing: I didn't know the answer. 'I've thought about being a personal trainer, or maybe something where I could help people, a fireman or a policeman, something like that,' I added.

'Really? Well, I've seen what you're going to do and it doesn't seem like any of those things to me.' She saw my surprise and smiled.

'What do you mean you've "seen" what I'm going to do?' I wanted to know more. It's not every day you get your career mapped out for you by your grandmother, and I was struggling to see a clear path.

She looked into the middle distance. 'I can see you just there … You look quite presentable with a nice suit and a good pair of shoes on …'

Up to that point I'd never owned a suit. I was agog!

'I can see you standing in front of a lot of people and you're talking to them and they're listening to every word you're saying. You're on a platform or a stage and there are other people as well, but they're watching you. You have something in your hand, but I can't tell what it is ...'

Her face scrunched up in frustration, and mine with curiosity.

When Nain explained her vision to me, I didn't know how to react.

I'd never enjoyed school and Nain knew this. Before I'd started at my comprehensive school I'd known it had a reputation as one of the roughest in the city, and I soon found out why. It became apparent very quickly that some of the teachers couldn't control their classes. At primary school there had been a sense among the pupils that 'I don't really want to be at school but I need to be here or I'll get into a lot of trouble.' At my comprehensive it was different: 'I don't want to be here but I can get away with showing my displeasure at being here. Nothing and no one is going to stop me.' It was chaos. There was fighting, throwing things in class and all sorts of misbehaviour. The dog-eat-dog life of the classrooms didn't suit me at all.

Part of me wanted to think about the future and what I was going to do when I grew up, but another part didn't care. My self-discipline had gone and with it my direction in life. All of a sudden I didn't know where I was going.

The only thing about school that interested me was the after-school martial-arts lessons I attended. Kung fu helps with all-round fitness and suppleness, confidence and self-esteem. It teaches you how to breathe properly and how to distribute energy around your body so that you can use it effectively. Whichever kung fu discipline you follow, you get a complete body (and mind) workout, but I practised wing chun. Buddhist monks used it as a means of self-defence – never attack – in their daily lives. For them it was about repetition, as well as allying movement with breathing and energy with thought, until the moves became almost a reflex action. I was awarded a junior black belt when I was eleven, and was developing the skills quicker than most other boys in the class. I had a knack for picking things up quickly.

As I progressed in martial arts I didn't know then that I was taking my first steps into the world of meditation. I found that the repetitive physical movements helped clear my mind so that I could focus on what I was doing without any distraction. This skill became invaluable to me later in life.

But in terms of my career I had no clear idea of what I was going to do. My comprehensive school wasn't conducive to learning or planning my life. So, I was astonished when Nain told me she'd had a vision of me standing on a stage and addressing lots of people. I had to try to understand.

What had she just said? And, more to the point, how had she 'seen' all this? Standing smartly dressed in front of a crowd of people who were hanging on my every word ... Was I going to become a stand-up comedian? A singer? Instinctively I knew I'd be neither – I couldn't sing and had never had a desire to go up on a stage and tell jokes. I pressed Nain for more but she said that was all she had seen, and when I asked what she had meant by 'seeing' such things, she told me that one day an image had popped into her mind, like a dream.

I knew exactly what she meant. I'd been having that kind of vision for years, but only time would tell whether hers would come true, like mine often did.

Nain was around eighty when I was fourteen, and had been a constant in my life since I could remember. I had lived through my formative years in her house, sleeping in the same room as her. Mum and Dad got back together when I was six, and my first brother Todd was born when I was ten. Ever since my mum and I had moved out to live with my dad, I had spent a few nights each week with Nain and my grandfather. She was a huge part of my life, so I noticed straight away when something was wrong.

It was around Christmas that year when she started to eat less and complained of feeling sick all the time. We noticed she had lost a bit of weight too, and by January there was obviously something very wrong with her. This wasn't just a bug or her being off her food. Nain had been a nurse, so perhaps she knew she needed to go to hospital. Most of us put off visiting the doctor when we're ill, but Nain felt so poorly that something had to be done. My mum took her to get checked out, and we waited on tenterhooks for the results of the tests they carried out on her.

I was pretty certain that Nain couldn't be in any serious trouble, so when the diagnosis came – cancer of the stomach and oesophagus – we were all devastated. I was extremely upset and in a complete daze. I didn't know what to do or say. It was like my heart had been wrenched out and the foundations of my life were crumbling beneath my feet. But as the days went by I noticed my emotions changing.

I was somehow managing to stay strangely detached from the situation. I still went to school and my routine didn't alter. Perhaps I was retreating into my own little safety zone. Everyone reacts differently to news like that. I remember doing a lot of thinking. I thought about how my grandfather would be feeling. He'd been with Nain for more than forty years, ever since they'd first met just after the war at a cinema in Anglesey. And what about my mum? She was extremely emotional and couldn't stop crying, so that gave me an immediate answer. We were all suffering inside, but Mum let her emotions show. She and Nain were so close. They were mother and daughter, but also, somehow, sisters and best friends too. Of course Mum was upset.

The cancer explained why Nain had been off her food, but we expected, with treatment, to have her around for a couple more years. It wasn't to be. Her condition worsened quickly, and she got weaker. We had to revise our prognosis from a couple of years down to a couple of months. When our physical bodies get older conditions like Nain's tend to hit hard, and Nain was in her eighties. Soon we were revising the couple of months to a couple of weeks. She had fallen ill in December, was diagnosed two months later in February and was now in hospital with only weeks to live.

This can't be happening, I kept thinking. It was the first time that a close relative had been so ill and the first time I'd had to face up to death. I found everything surreal, and despite the quick turn of events, my world seemed to be turning in slow motion. It wasn't just my Nain's condition I was thinking about, it was my own mortality. Nain's cancer had made me think again about what happens to us after death, and I was confronted with the realization that none of us is on this earth for ever. People I'd thought indestructible were clearly nothing of the sort, and if they weren't, I certainly wasn't.

But I also felt a curious sense of calm. The spiritual things that had happened to me had instilled in me the belief that there was something after death, so when Nain passed she would still be around. Somehow, somewhere, she would still be there. Turmoil mixed with calm and knowing, an odd combination.

I attended school less and less. I'd stay up late, sleep in and then do whatever I liked. I couldn't face the chaos. I just couldn't. I needed to retreat. I needed time on my own. I made sure I went in just often enough to keep me out of serious trouble, but my life was spinning out of control. There was nothing for me at school – there never really had been – and everything I knew at home that was good and pure and safe was about to come crashing down. Some people might argue that going to school would have been a good way to keep my mind occupied, but they weren't at my school. The constant pressure there would have made me feel worse. So I stayed away as much as I could.

Instead I spent long days in bed or playing computer games until it was time to go and visit Nain in hospital. I used to sit in the café at the hospital to eat a burger or a packet of salt-and-vinegar peanuts before I went in to see her. It's funny the kind of details you remember about times of crisis, but there I was, getting a quick bite before I went up to Nain's ward for a few hours.

I used to hold her hand and talk about the kind of day I'd had. She'd ask me how school was and I'd say, 'Fine.' We both knew that wasn't true, but the time for caring about school and everyday things had long gone. She asked me to help her tidy her hair because she still wanted to look nice in front of the other women in the ward who, if I'm honest, had lost their marbles or were too ill to notice anything. So I would comb her hair and talk to her about mundane things. That was all I could talk about. I didn't know what else I was supposed to say.

The situation was unreal. I still hadn't quite grasped how ill Nain was or what was going to happen. Or perhaps I had but I refused to believe it. No matter, I made sure – whether I'd been to school or not – that I was at the hospital every day, visiting Nain and bringing in the things she'd asked for or helping her with whatever she needed to do.

My grandfather was there every day, too, but my dad was at the hospital next door. There was a good reason for this: in the Princess Anne Hospital, which is literally next door to Southampton General, my mum was giving birth to another baby.

It's an almost impossible situation to get your head around, so you can imagine how we all felt. My mum and dad had announced that they were going to have a third child several months earlier, just before Nain had fallen ill. When her test results had revealed that she was terminally ill, Mum was heavily pregnant. Joy and devastation in equal measures, all at once, in the same family. It was difficult to know how to feel: Nain would depart this earth and my mum's new baby would enter it at much the same time.

We divided the visiting duties between us. I would be with Nain while my dad was with Mum. My poor grandfather spent time with his wife, then went to see his daughter. It must have been torture for Mum to know that her own mother was gravely ill at the hospital next door while she was unable to do anything about it. I can't imagine how that must have felt. I just knew I had to be with Nain and comfort her in any way I could. But it was clear that she was deteriorating almost by the hour. She was being violently sick every fifteen minutes or so, which exhausted her. It was hard to watch. One day, between the bouts of vomiting, she looked up at me with clear eyes and an expression that said a thousand words. She couldn't speak but those eyes still shone. There was so much warmth and love in them, but that unforgettable expression told me she didn't have long left and knew it.

During my daily visits we had skirted around the issue and stuck to chatting about what I had been doing. But in that wordless moment she told me everything I needed to know. We didn't have to say anything about her condition. She knew. I knew. And as she looked up at me with those kind, beautiful eyes she was saying goodbye. I will never forget that moment, or the look in her eyes.

Word soon reached us that my mum had gone into labour in the hospital next door. Nain had expressly said she wanted to see the baby and, as you can imagine, my mum was desperate for her to see her newborn child. She was also desperate to see her mother.

My mum gave birth to a healthy baby boy, called Kian, on 23 February 2006. There had been health scares recently so the doctors wouldn't allow her to take him to visit his grandmother until the next morning.

Even though my mum had had a Caesarean and was very weak, she was determined to see her mother and introduce the new arrival to her.

Kian was quite a big baby, and as soon as Nain – who was awake when they arrived the next morning – saw him, she said, 'Oh, wow, he's a real buster!' and in the brief time they got to spend together she was calling him Buster Bartlett. We all laughed, but our smiles were tinged with sadness.

With both Nain and Mum very weak, the family reunion was cut short, and my tearful mum had to go back to Princess Anne's. But the main thing was that Nain got to meet Kian. Soon afterwards Mum and Dad named him Kian Buster Bartlett.

That day in late February was one that none of us would ever forget. After Mum had gone back next door, I was with Nain all the time, but then news reached us that Mum had passed out and needed a blood transfusion. The doctors were looking after her and there was nothing we could do, so my grandfather, my uncle and I stayed with Nain. That afternoon she stopped being sick so much, and had stopped talking. Soon she had shut her eyes, and was breathing deeply. This was how it started. As she lay there, not speaking, with her eyes closed and her husband holding her hand, she stopped breathing. That was when the nurse came.

It was unlike anything I'd experienced before, and as the tears rolled down my face, I saw that my grandfather

and uncle – strong men who didn't normally show much
emotion – were crying too. And there, lying on the bed,
was Nain. She had looked after me, told me stories
and been so kind to me throughout my life. And, more
importantly, she had understood. She had understood
everything. And now she was half a world away.

New Beginnings

Out of death came life, and in the
immediate aftermath of Nain's passing I went to visit
my mum — and my little brother Kian, of course. Mum
was very weak still, and very sad that her mother had died
in the adjacent hospital only twenty-four hours earlier.
Perhaps she even felt a little guilty that she hadn't been
there at the last.

Me? I was still in a daze. Soon after I'd seen Nain
take her last breath I'd wandered down the corridor to
the lift to go home, existing in some sort of limbo.
My head was flooded with the experience I had just
witnessed. In the car on the way home the radio was on
but I wasn't listening to it. Instead I looked out at the
people on the streets of Southampton. There were gangs
of youths hanging around, a couple holding hands,
people coming in and out of pubs and restaurants,
everything you would expect to see in a busy city on any
week night. Life went on. Time ticked by. It didn't stop
for anyone. I saw the glare of the streetlamps and passing
headlights. At that moment life was a blur, and I felt as if I
didn't belong. I was numb to everything and couldn't wait
to get home. I was utterly exhausted mentally.

I went back with my grandfather to his house for some peace and quiet but also because I was sure he needed company. Dad had been with Mum and Kian, but then had had to come home to look after Todd. So that night I was back at the house where I'd spent so much of my childhood, and as I climbed into bed I became aware that the room I was to sleep in had been Nain's. I wasn't afraid or flooded with memories of Nain: as soon as my head hit the pillow I fell asleep. I was exhausted, and the events of the past few weeks had finally caught up with me. We had spent a lot of time in those hospitals over the past few days, which had taken its toll on me. I hadn't realized how tired I was and slept deeply until late the next morning, in the room where Nain had told me her stories. It still felt warm and welcoming, but one thing was different. My Nain wasn't there physically any more.

My mum couldn't make it to the funeral in Anglesey because she was still recovering from her own physical ordeal. My dad stayed with her, so the same three men who had been with Nain when she passed over – myself, my grandfather and my uncle – journeyed up to Wales. I'd been asked if I wanted to go. There was no way I was going to say no, so off I went. In some ways I felt an extra responsibility because I would be representing my immediate family, with my mum and dad at home. For a fourteen-year-old this was pretty grown-up stuff, but I absolutely had to go and wouldn't have missed it.

The night before we left, I slept badly. There were so many things going around in my head. By now it had been a week or so since Nain had died and I had had a chance to think about what had happened. I was incredibly sad and felt pain in my heart as I settled into the back seat of the car for the journey. Thinking about Nain and her passing made me understand how much I loved her and how much I was going to miss her, and already I felt a huge hole in my life where she had been.

Six hours later we arrived in Wales. We were to stay with one of my aunts, and the service was to be held at a church in the middle of nowhere. It stood next to a farm and overlooked fields with sheep and bare hedgerows.

We had picked out a headstone with the undertakers – who were, incidentally, connected to the family – and we were ready. I remember going to the funeral of my dad's mum, Gladys, when I was very young. My mum was very upset, so much so that I had to comfort her throughout the service. Mum wasn't there this time, and because I was on my own and felt responsible I didn't want to succumb to emotion. I wanted to keep it together. Hold it, hold it, hold it, I kept thinking, but when Nain's coffin was lowered into her grave I couldn't hold on any longer. I remember looking down into the hole in the ground and tears welling up. The fact that I was part of the funeral party and holding one of the ropes at the time meant I couldn't wipe my eyes. Big, bursting tears fell as the coffin went down.

After we'd seen some great-aunts,
uncles and cousins in Wales, we went back home, and it
was time to restart my life. To say that was difficult would
be an understatement. I took a long time to settle back
into any sort of routine, and my mum was still dreadfully
upset. Nain's passing had devastated everybody and the
thought of going back to school just didn't appeal to me.
If anything, I hated the place even more, and when I did go
in, it just didn't seem relevant to me after everything that
had happened. In fact, I remember feeling angry at being
made to go in the mornings and my reaction to lessons
was far more aggressive. English? Who cared? Maths?
Stuff it! It was if Nain's passing had tipped me over the
edge as far as school was concerned. Over the course of
the next year my appearance record was not exemplary.

Life slowly got back to some sort of normality, but
Mum was still grieving deeply for Nain, and missed her
desperately. About four months after Nain had passed,
Mum sprang something on me that took me completely
by surprise.

'Ross … how do you fancy coming with me to a
spiritualist church?'

'A spiritualist what, Mum?' I had never heard of a
spiritualist church.

'It's a place where … where people can try and get in
touch with spirits in the afterlife.'

I pondered her request for a few seconds. Suddenly it
became clear. 'You want to try and get in touch with Nain.'

'Yes, Ross, I do. I feel like I've got to try. Do you want to come with me? Just the once? I don't want to go alone.'

She explained that she had seen mediums and psychics before I was born and this wasn't something to be feared. She assured me it would be an interesting experience, and if we managed to get through to Nain it would be worthwhile. I decided to go with her, mainly to give her some support, but also because I was curious.

As we walked up to Shirley Spiritualist Church I thought what an unassuming building it was. It looked like a bungalow, and was wedged between a maroon garage and some houses on a relatively quiet suburban road. Opposite there was a health centre. It was not the glittering palace I had thought appropriate to a place where you could contact those who had passed over.

Once we got inside the smallish building, I was struck by the relaxed and welcoming atmosphere. It was like a mini church with a little stand for the hymn numbers and an altar or rostrum at the front. It wasn't so weird. Mum and I took seats halfway down one of the aisles and waited for the service to begin. You could tell how much Mum was hoping – straining – to be chosen by the medium because she was sitting up straight with her eyes fixed towards the front, holding her hands tightly into her waist.

When the medium came out I watched her closely as the chairman welcomed everybody to the church, said a few prayers and introduced her. Her big, friendly smile drew us all in, and she spoke with soft authority.

The audience – there were almost thirty people in attendance – was hanging on her every word. The expectation in the air was almost palpable, and as the medium shut her eyes, I sensed that everyone in the room was willing her to come to them with information or contact with a recently deceased loved one.

My mum was one of those people. She so dearly wanted the medium to bring forward Nain, and we sat through one connection after another, hoping that the next one would be for us. But it never was – the medium made connection after connection but not with Nain. I watched people nod in acknowledgement when the medium revealed information about their loved ones, and I saw the comfort it gave them.

I was fascinated by the medium's mannerisms and how she was communicating with spirits. There was a pause between each of her sentences, and I studied the way she seemed to be having a private conversation with someone who wasn't there before she turned to address us. As I was gazing into the middle distance, wondering what it all meant, I became aware of a silence in the room and the medium was looking at me.

Then she said: 'You had some experiences as a child.'

Not a question, a statement. The woman at the end of Mum's bed, the glowing hand shape outside the glass door and the moving glass were suddenly in my mind. How could she know this? I'd never met her before or been to this place. I hadn't even known it existed.

'Yeah.' I nodded slowly, aware that everyone in the room was now staring at me. 'Yeah ... yeah, I have,' I repeated.

'You know, in the future you could be doing something very similar to what I'm doing now.' She smiled and returned to the conversations she was having with I-didn't-know-who, then went on to the next person.

Hold on a minute, I wanted to say. What do you mean, I could be up there doing what you're doing in the future? How did you know I'd had experiences as a child? And why haven't you brought Nain through yet? That's what we've come for! But there were no answers to those questions, not that night anyway.

We left the church frustrated, and me feeling a bit 'What just happened there?' I had no idea, but I wanted to know why the medium had picked on me and why she had said the things she did. What had she seen in me? Why was I singled out?

After that we went to more public demonstrations in different churches. My mum had been bitten by the bug and she wasn't going to stop until Nain had contacted us or we had contacted her (at that point I still wasn't sure which way round these things worked). But the outcome was always the same – no contact from Nain. My mum was disappointed, but I enjoyed seeing the mediums in action. It was also a nice way to spend some time hanging out with my mum, and for her it was a little break from looking after baby Kian.

During one of the demonstrations at the church in Shirley – there are several spiritualist churches in the Southampton area – we were preparing ourselves for another Nainless night when the medium broke off from a reading and turned to me. Mum and I were sitting near the front, to his left, and he looked down towards me.

'I've got to talk to you,' he said. 'I see that you could work as a medium yourself. You have this ability. You have this gift. And you could do it full-time if you wanted to.'

'Erm ...' I didn't know what to say in front of a roomful of people waiting to be connected to a dear departed loved one. I felt a bit embarrassed.

'I can see all this for you,' he continued. 'All the best.'

He turned back to the crowd and carried on with the demonstration. I won't tell you what I said to myself, but it was along the lines of 'What the ...!' My mum was looking at me in a funny way, but my mind was whirring. I immediately thought back to what Nain had told me shortly before she passed over, that she had seen me standing in front of a large crowd with a suit on and everyone listening to me intently. I didn't know what she had meant at the time, but now two separate mediums had told me more or less the same thing. Was this what Nain had seen? Perhaps it was. I was still surprised by the attention, but something was beginning to stir inside me. That two different mediums in Shirley had broken off from their demonstrations to single me out couldn't have been mere coincidence. But the thought of getting up in front of loads of people and talking like those mediums did was terrifying.

Back then I had little self-confidence, and the idea of being put on the spot like that – with so many people expecting so much from one person – did not appeal to me. I'd been to a few public demonstrations now and I knew you had to think on your feet. Even comedians get to rehearse their routines beforehand, I thought, but the mediums looked as though they had no idea what was going to happen next or who they were going to speak to. Me up there doing it? No, thank you!

Because of our quest to get in touch with Nain, we ended up going to Shirley every week. We still got nothing from her, but my growing interest in the whole thing and, of course, the comments from the mediums had piqued my curiosity. Then, during another demonstration, when the medium chirped up, 'You have a gift ... You can do this too, if you want to,' I decided it was time to find out what those people were talking about.

I'd resisted until then, just taking things on board and not really talking about it to anyone or pursuing it, mainly because I was still trying to process what had been said and what it might mean. Now it was time to take a deep breath and find out what was what. I wasn't sure how to go about it – did I just search them out after a demonstration and ask, 'By the way, that thing you said about me'?

One evening the opportunity presented itself to me. By now Mum and I had got to know a few people at the

Shirley church. We were becoming familiar faces too, so it wasn't unusual for someone to smile or say hello to us. After a demonstration someone asked us if we fancied coming to a meditation evening the following week. It would be slightly different from the usual public demonstration, they said, but we were welcome to come along and it would be an interesting experience. We decided to go. It was being hosted by a medium who came from out of town.

I had, of course, heard of meditation, but I wasn't sure what went into it or how it worked, so this gathering, I thought, would be an education. My mum was still waiting patiently for some sort of contact with Nain, and this was something slightly different from what we had already tried. It was worth a shot. A change is as good as a rest, they say.

When we got there, the hostess, who was in her early sixties, welcoming and friendly, was explaining what meditation was and that we would be doing a guided meditation. She would tell us how to get into the zone and how to quiet the mind. And, more importantly, she'd help us throughout the process.

The idea of making my mind still was difficult for me to comprehend. With all the thinking I liked to do, this seemed to me to be pretty much impossible. But then a thought – yes, another thought – struck me. I had been used to blocking things out when I was practising my martial arts. I used the physical movement to get to a stage

where my mind was completely still and I was moving
without thinking. Maybe that was what she meant.

The medium asked us to sit in a certain way – legs like
this, on a chair like that, in a comfortable position, hands
on your lap, shut your eyes – and then to follow what she
was saying. Feel the weight of your body, feel the air on
your skin, feel the tension release … Say the word 'soft',
think about the images that word makes in your mind,
bring that word to the areas of tension. Notice how the
muscles respond to the thought. Feel how relaxed you're
becoming. Words, images and sensations all together.
Now say those words, let go in your mind and see what
images come to you that are associated with the words.
Feel the sensations of 'soft' and let go. See the images
and feel the sensations. Feel how they spread around
the body, from the forehead to the jaw, down to the
shoulders and into the ribcage. Everything becomes soft.
Everything is let go.

After a few more minutes of her prompts, I felt
relaxed and totally calm. I was enjoying the feelings those
words seemed to generate. She then asked us to imagine
walking along a pathway through a lush forest, to carry
on walking, taking in the sights, sounds and feelings this
little walk inside our minds would produce. We were now
on our own, around half a dozen of us sitting in a circle,
each engrossed in our own little worlds.

It wasn't long before my experience became
incredibly vivid, a full 'wow'. She had explained before

she set us on this forest pathway that whatever we saw or felt was okay. Just go with whatever you see, and feel what happens.

As I was walking down my forest pathway, I noticed it was night time and there were stars in the sky above the trees. I was also aware that there was an eye in the sky, looking down on me. It was suspended in mid-air, just watching me, as I walked down the forest path. As I saw the eye, I felt tingling and shivering down my right side and all across my back. It was lovely! But in my mind the eye was still watching me, and as I continued to walk a hand emerged out of the darkness. Not in a threatening way – it just opened its palm as I walked towards it. As I was about to explore what was going to happen next, the medium called us back into the real world, and I, like everyone else, opened my eyes and raised my eyebrows.

The harsh light of the hall made me blink once or twice, and I emerged from my first ever meditation saying to my mum, 'Well, that was different!'

While my visualizations were very vivid and had lots of things going on in them, Mum had said she'd had a very pleasant and relaxing experience. No eyes or hands emerging from the darkness, Mum? No.

The medium asked us how our experience had been, so I explained what had happened during my little walk in the forest.

'That's very interesting, Ross,' she said, with an inquisitive frown. 'You say this is the first time you've

meditated? Perhaps – and this is only a perhaps –
you've had a lot of psychic energy stored up there in
your head for quite some while. This sounds like the first
time you've had any sort of release, and really tapped
into energy of this type. You might just have tapped into
something there!'

That I might have a gift was being suggested once
again by the hostess of the meditation group. Everything
was beginning to make sense.

'Let's not get ahead of ourselves yet, but these results
are certainly very vivid for someone who has never
meditated before.'

'So what do I do now?'

'Well, if your mum's okay with it and you're up for
it, I think you should come along to the next gathering.
It's for people who have the same sort of ability to see
things as you have. In the workshop we try to hone the
meditation skill, then learn to harness and control it so
we can do readings, or whatever we want to do with it.'

I was not quite fifteen, and I was being told that I had
the ability to see things. After one meditation! This time,
though, not only was someone telling me there might
be more to this than met the eye, but I also had evidence
of a kind. I had just seen some incredibly vivid things in
my meditation visualization, so perhaps the mediums
– and Nain – had been right. Or, at least, they were on to
something. I had to find out for sure, so I didn't hesitate
to sign up for the workshop. I needed some answers.

Up to that point I had been happy to go with the flow, and was even indifferent. I didn't question my early experiences. A lot of people would, but I'm very laid-back so I accepted them and carried on as usual. They became a normal part of my life. School was the same: I merely existed and survived, not really caring where I was going or what was going on. But this was different. I was intrigued. I needed more. I wanted to see where it took me. For the first time in my life I wanted to initiate something, to explore. And this seemed to be the perfect way in which to do that.

I turned up at Shirley for the next gathering not really knowing what to expect. Mum was by my side (as ever) so I wasn't nervous. In fact, I was looking forward to seeing how the session would progress. The last one had been a bit of an eye-opener, and if that was anything to go by I was eager to see what this one would produce. I was hoping for more clear dream-like visuals.

We walked into the hall and found half a dozen people there, all women and all aged between forty and fifty. I was by far the youngest and a teenage boy to boot. But I didn't feel too out of place: everyone was friendly and the medium who had headed the last guided meditation was there again, ready to help us into whatever realms we were to explore.

And so it started. We sat in a circle and got relaxed. We did the same meditations, with the medium guiding us through them. I was totally calm. She asked us to imagine a 'meditation room' – a place where something (or someone) would be waiting for us when we got there.

Often in meditations – especially with a guide – you're asked to go on a journey. You might be asked to imagine yourself in a valley with a stream running through it, or standing at the top of a hill looking down at a pathway. The medium at this gathering liked to use the forest visualization, using the path through it as a visual metaphor for going deeper and deeper into the meditative state. The more you 'walk' and the deeper you go, the more tuned in to psychic energy you become. Then images in your mind start to come through clearer and more vividly. They might be anything, and the important thing, the medium was keen to tell us, was not to judge but just be aware of the images that popped up.

At the end of a walk through a forest or along a river or down a hill, or whatever the visualization might be, you're asked to imagine a door and to walk through it into a room, which will often contain something of significance. I was feeling relaxed and my forest visualization had become more and more vivid when we were asked to imagine the room.

'Now you've entered the room, I'd like you to tell me what you see,' the medium said.

I had entered my 'room' and I was immediately aware of a presence or a shadow standing next to me, like when you're doing the washing-up and someone walks up to you softly. You don't turn around because your hands are full and dripping with soap suds, but you know someone is there. It's not a threatening presence, just a feeling that something or someone is behind you. That was how I felt in my meditation room. Someone was standing behind me. Right behind me.

Then I heard something. A name. William. It wasn't a whisper or a shout, but clear speech. A bit like the names I had heard in my head from time to time as I had been growing up. But there it was: William. It was as if this presence was telling me its name.

'Is anybody getting anything?' asked the medium.

'I am,' I answered quietly, with the images and sounds still fixed in my head and my eyes closed. 'I feel a presence beside me in the room. I can hear a name. William.'

'Well done, Ross,' she said. 'That's very interesting. Can anybody take a man in the spirit world by the name of William?'

I opened my eyes slightly and to my amazement saw that the woman next to me had put her hand up.

'Good. Good.' The medium smiled. 'Ross, I want you to shut your eyes again and try to find out who that person was close to.'

'But how do I do that?' I asked. 'I don't know how or what to do next.'

'Go back to your room, Ross, and see if William is still there. Ask him in your mind. Don't question what you're seeing or hearing. Let it all happen naturally. Be patient. Just ask the question and you'll get the answer.'

I closed my eyes again, and imagined myself back in the meditation room. Thankfully, the presence was still standing beside me. It didn't have a shape or a form, but I felt it – or he – was there.

'Can you tell me anything more about you, William?' I asked silently. 'Anything at all would be good.'

As soon as I asked the question I got … feelings. They weren't words or sounds, just feelings. As these feelings came through I felt completely confident, both mentally and physically, almost on a high. The feelings indicated that he was a strong character, a strong person in life. I explained them aloud to the lady sitting next to me, and she said, yes, those had been William's character traits when he was alive in this world. He had been a strong man, someone you could depend on.

I went back into my mind and, without even asking, an image of a trilby hat came through – it just appeared. It started off as a thought, then I heard, 'Trilby.' I said it aloud and it was taken and understood by the lady sitting next to me. I went back into the room and asked William what he had done and how he had passed. I got the feeling that he'd had trouble walking, and then a thought came to my mind, as if someone was saying, 'My knees weren't that good.' After I had repeated aloud the information given to me, the woman said, yes, just before he passed away he couldn't really walk about much as his legs were very painful.

Just as I was about to go back and ask him some more questions – I was getting into it and enjoying the experience – the medium said, 'Right. I think we'll leave it there now.'

Everyone stretched and adjusted their seating and there were murmurs in the circle. They all looked at me. The medium saw my disappointment.

'Don't worry, Ross.' She smiled. 'I know you wanted to explore more, but be patient. There'll be plenty of time to go deeper into this. But I have to say . . .' she paused '. . . I knew after your first meditation experience that there was something special about you. You seemed to take to it very quickly, and the speed at which you're able to clear your mind and focus is really impressive. Stick with it, because you can go far. Now, I know the rest of you are looking at Ross and thinking, Why can't I see what Ross is seeing? The same applies to everyone: each one of you is different and the way you tap into psychic energy will be different. So if you didn't experience anything tonight, don't worry … It will come.'

I didn't know what to say. I was still fourteen, and this was only the second time I had meditated, yet it wasn't the first time someone had told me they saw me progressing in this area. Add to this Nain telling me she had seen me onstage … That little vision was gathering meaning. What if she had seen me being a medium? What if all the people hanging on my every word had been there to connect with their loved ones after they had passed over?

The idea was mind-boggling to me, because I still didn't quite understand what had happened to me during those two meditation sessions. I seemed to slip effortlessly into the meditative state that the medium had guided us into, and once I was in it, images, thoughts, feelings and even sounds just sprang up without my thinking about them. Maybe there was something in what people had told me. Maybe I really should explore this more.

All I knew, as I walked away from the gathering that evening, was that I had given my first ever reading.

The Psychic
Circle

'*What should I do now?*' I asked the
medium, after the meditation workshop.

'You need to find yourself a circle.' She smiled,
warmly. 'A group of people who sit together with one
express purpose: to help someone develop whatever
gifts and abilities they might have. It's almost like a very
intimate school.'

I was fourteen and had attended just two meditation
gatherings. Even though they had been a success, I
had the impression that I lacked full control over the
thoughts and images. Although the medium was guiding
us through the meditations and I was putting some
questions to whoever or whatever I happened to come
across in my visualizations, I still wasn't quite sure
what to do when I got to that state. As the number of my
experiences grew, I started to wonder if there was a way
I could guide myself into the meditative state, tap into
any psychic energy faster, and whether I could direct
conversations with the spirits I met to get sharper,
more accurate information from them.

'So, what do you say, Ross? How do you feel about joining a circle? It might do wonders for your abilities. You could really develop them once you're in one.'

I wanted to say yes, but there was a problem: the church had strict rules and guidelines when it came to age. I was simply too young to join one. That was where Mum stepped in. She'd been with me at every workshop, every demonstration and every trip to a spiritualist church. She was still waiting for contact with Nain, but my sudden rapid development had taken over. Now she had to fight my corner with the church so that I could join a circle. The first thing to do was to find out who was running the show, and because we were familiar faces around the place now, that didn't take long. His name was Cliff, and he became the most important person in my early spiritual development.

He was in his seventies, always very friendly, with an approachable, encouraging manner, and he often chaired meetings when the regular medium wasn't available. One day Mum introduced herself to him. It seemed I was getting a bit of a reputation in the church because he had heard of my progress. When we met, I told him what had happened during my meditations and that I had been told to find a circle. There was no time to waste so I asked him straight out whether there was any chance of joining one of the circles at the church.

'I'm not sure, Ross,' he said. 'You're so young and the church has strict rules on that sort of thing. The only way

I could see you joining one is if your mum was with you. I'll have to go away and think about it.'

Cliff had a reputation for being opinionated and a bit of a rule-breaker. Although he had a kind face and was open and friendly, we had heard stories about his straight talking and willingness to take risks. Apparently his personality and approach hadn't always sat comfortably with the other church members. Luckily for us, his maverick side shone through and he informed me that I was free to join a circle, as long as Mum accompanied me as chaperone to every meeting and kept a close eye on me.

I attended my first circle at the church and it was a lot like the meditation sessions I had been to, but because there were only six or seven of us, it had an intimacy that hadn't existed there. As before, I was the youngest member by far, but again this didn't bother me. By this stage I knew a few people, so I felt at ease and, as Cliff sat down and took charge, quite excited. I had no idea what would happen in these meetings and couldn't wait to get started.

First he asked what everyone present had experienced. When I reeled off my experiences at Nain and Grandfather's house, as well as all that had happened in the meditation sessions, Cliff raised both eyebrows. 'Wow!' He chuckled. 'That really is quite something!'

We had a bit of laugh – they weren't used to having a fourteen-year-old in their circle, especially not one who had experienced so many random events. I laughed because it had been a crazy journey for me. I wasn't sure how I'd got there but I was sitting in a psychic circle. It was like being in some secret club, and it was difficult to get my head around. I didn't feel pressured because they were all nice people and the meditations I had done had been pleasant experiences. They hadn't scared me … they were actually very relaxing. But I still wanted answers. I wanted to know how far I could take this, and I had a feeling the circle would help me and that it was the best place to find out.

Cliff guided us in a short, basic meditation, the like of which I was now familiar with. Even during the warm-up I was getting feelings coming through. Feelings of presences observing me. I didn't know who they were or what they were doing there, but I was soon to learn. Cliff made sure of that.

After that first circle meeting at the church, Cliff called to tell me that he wanted to start a private circle at his home and that I was more than welcome to join in. This meant breaking away from the church. It turned out that he had had a falling-out with some of the members – his bluntness had rubbed a few people up the wrong way – and wanted to move the circle somewhere else. I'm sure this move didn't help his cause, but I liked his no-nonsense manner and decided to accept his offer, although I was grateful to the church for everything it had introduced me to. It didn't matter to me or the rest of us where we meditated or went through our exercises.

It made sense to go with Cliff. He had been good to me so far and encouraged me whenever he could, and he had also bent a few rules to allow me to join the circle.

When I turned up at his house, I discovered that he'd turned his garage into a room fitted out specifically for the circle. There it was: a dedicated place for us to learn in. There was a table in the centre of the room with chairs arranged around it. To the side was a smaller table, which held other items that we might find useful during our sessions, including water, candles and crystals. Any light from outside the room was blacked out and the lighting inside the garage was subtle. It felt like an alternative night school; a more private version of the circle we had been in at the church. The fact that I had been selected for this little group made me feel ready to take things to the next level. I still wasn't sure what this would mean, but I felt I was moving in some sort of direction and that there was a natural momentum I didn't want to fight. So it was decided. Every Monday night at seven o'clock the others in the circle and I, with Mum, would gather in Cliff's converted garage and go to work.

With only a dimly lit candle to illuminate the room, the mood was always just right, and in that special ambience we were free to experiment, to learn and strengthen our skills. Some teenagers have a tutor to help them in the lead-up to their exams, and I was doing the same sort of thing, but this was a private psychic circle, and I was studying to become a better medium and improve the ways in which I would contact the spirit world. I could handle these lessons. Unlike schoolwork, they were fun and soon I was progressing in ways I couldn't have imagined.

Unlike the early meditation session at the church, the shackles were off. Everything was geared to giving readings and strengthening our connections to the spirit world. We were encouraged to link up as often as we could, and Cliff taught us specific meditations to connect with the spirit world. His guided meditations required us to think about walking along a beach, sitting in a cave or tramping through mountains. They all helped us to relax, as we imagined how they looked, smelt, felt and even sounded.

I learnt that through meditation and visualization I could link up quickly and tap into energies that would allow me almost to have an extended conversation with someone who wanted to get in touch. I also learnt that when it came to contacting the spirit world, everything hinges on the intention. We learnt meditations, breath work and a visualization in which I had to see in my mind a beam of light, which I would send upwards to the spirit world. Inside the beam there would be a series of intentions: I would ask the spirit world for the best contact possible, clear connection, and vivid evidential information. The more you ask for in meditation, the more you get back, and this was the most important lesson I learnt in Cliff's circle from the outset.

We would do our meditations and visualizations in the flickering candlelight and once we'd finished we'd report back and chat about what we had experienced.

As a medium, when you want to get into that zone and use the psychic power to connect with the spirit world, intention is your key. Within your meditations you visualize what you want to achieve: getting closer to the spirit world and strengthening the connection. But I learnt there are many meditations for many different purposes.

Cliff guided us through the meditations, his voice softening as he asked us to imagine a certain scenario, and steered us from one part of the visualization to the next. They quickly became exercises that were more a journey of experience. We would imagine one scenario, then another and another. In each one we would go on a journey: we would be asked to imagine walking from one place to another, down steps into a cave or deeper into a forest where the trees would get denser, and be receptive to what was in there, whether it was an object or a colour or an overriding feeling.

We did other meditations in which the aim was the complete opposite – not to think, but to go to that quiet space and hold our minds there. Making my mind go still was the hardest part, and I quickly found that the only way to get to that state of stillness is by practice. Once you get there it's an amazingly relaxing feeling, which sparks off all kinds of physical sensations like shivers and tingles.

Through these private circle sessions, I learnt that meditation is about connecting to your inner self and the different levels of energy all around us. It focuses the mind – and the more focused the mind, the better you can communicate with the spirit world. We all have thoughts that come in and out of our heads all the time, but the more we focus, the further we can go into that zone, and the less those random thoughts creep in. As I said before, it may sound difficult but practice makes perfect. And that was what Cliff's circles allowed me to do: to practise hard without interruption, in an encouraging environment.

On top of meditations, we would experiment with various exercises that were specifically designed to make the best connection to the spirit world. For example, one member of the circle would be asked to hold a ribbon and – using the intention meditation – try to transfer energy into the material, then pass it around. By touching the ribbon and using our intuition, we could feel what the person who had put their energy into it was feeling. The circle members didn't know each other well – we certainly didn't socialize outside the circle because we all had very different lives, and intuiting someone's psychic energy in the ribbon tested how well we could pick up on feelings. Not quite psychometry, but it was similar.

In another exercise Cliff would hand us a flower that someone had brought with them that evening. He would tell us to use it as a tool to do a reading. We were asked to look at the flower, and use whatever information came through from the spirit world to tell the group not only whose flower it was, but also how that person was feeling and what they were happy or worried about. On one flower I had to read, I saw that half of its petals were wilting and some had fallen off. As I looked at it, a thought came to me that the person who owned it had a hair problem on one side of their head. When I relayed this information at the end of the exercise, a member of the circle popped up and said, yes, they had gone grey on one side and often combed the rest of their hair to hide it. That was how it worked: we'd hold the flower, concentrate on it and, depending on how it looked or what its energy was like, we divined information from it.

The flower-reading exercise proved quite fruitful. Sometimes, once I had meditated and tapped into the psychic energy that had been transferred into a flower, a spirit might step in and give me information or I might just get feelings, images and sounds from touching and looking at it.

If a member of the spirit world had shown himself or herself when I was holding a flower, they might guide me to a part of it that I wouldn't ordinarily have taken much notice of, giving it new meaning or significance. One such reading left me in a tricky situation. While I was holding the flower, a spirit made me aware of a black spot on it and a feeling that its owner had a 'black spot' on his or her body, something that shouldn't be there, like an infection. I wasn't sure how to relay this information because it was potentially upsetting.

There was silence in the room, and everyone was waiting for my reading. Slowly and haphazardly I explained what I had felt and seen.

A male voice in the flickering light said, 'Yes, it's mine.' It was Cliff's flower. My eyes widened and my eyebrows almost touched the ceiling in surprise.

'Did you ever have some sort of growth in the past?' I gulped, nervously. 'Something internal that shouldn't have been there?'

As I held my breath Cliff explained that he had had cancer in the past and that he was now well clear of it. Not only that but he said he was really impressed with the evidential information I had managed to take from the flower.

Cliff and I were getting close, and we often had conversations about his life and work, as well as discussing the best ways to connect to the spirit world. He had told me that although he had certain abilities he was more involved in the organizational side of things, and his forte was spiritual healing. Throughout his life he had dedicated himself to healing people using his own energy, giving readings and running circles to help others develop their abilities.

Cliff was very down-to-earth and wise. He really knew his stuff and had been connecting in different ways to the spirit world for a long, long time. He had had his own experiences but they weren't the sort to make you go, 'Wow!' He taught me how to conduct myself as a medium. He told me that a medium has to bring their own individuality to their work, that I should never be afraid to express my mannerisms and style during readings. He also taught me never to brag about what I did, but encouraged me to share my experiences and talk about them as long as there was a purpose in doing so. I am writing this book to share my experiences and explain my journey so far, as well as to show you that after we've passed there is something else. If I can, I want to help people.

Cliff also taught me to respect others and their lives, the spirit world and those who have passed into it. In his usual straight-talking way, he reminded me that as a medium I should remember my manners when I talk to people, that it was about caring, taking responsibility and being mature. I should aim to live a good life and practise what I preached. These weren't alien concepts to me, but at fourteen I had never taken much notice of anyone who had told me this before. But Cliff was different. He was like Obi-Wan Kenobi from the *Star Wars* films. A sage old Jedi Knight passing on information, secrets and teachings to an apprentice. I trusted his opinions and saw that he, for the most part, lived his life as I wanted to live mine. I respected his caring nature, and the way he looked out for others. He wasn't perfect and neither was I, but he always did his best, backed up by his spiritual beliefs.

He thought that the role of a medium should be much more than that of go-between: he or she was an integral part of society; a spiritual leader, counsellor and healer. This struck a chord with me. Suddenly I was in an environment where my experiences were starting to make sense and slot together. Not only that, but I was being encouraged to do more, to express myself in ways I had never dreamt of and to develop abilities that had always been lurking in the background. For the first time ever I felt mentally focused, physically strong and motivated. Every Monday night at Cliff's circle, I felt as though I was growing up.

At the circle we continued to use special objects to improve our awareness and connection to the spirit world. They get you used to working the intuitive and expressive parts of the mind that we don't use much in everyday life, opening up our thinking and strengthening the areas a medium needs most.

One of our exercises involved Tarot cards. Unlike most card-readers we didn't use them to predict the future. Instead we looked at the picture on the card we were given and used our intuition and connection to the spirit world to find out how it related to the person who had given it.

For instance, if there was a castle on the card with four towers, that meant something; if the image on the card showed a person looking away and out, that meant something too. With the castle card, I asked the spirit world what the image might mean and a thought came to me. Three of the four towers in the image were taller than the fourth: it might mean that the person who had given me the card had four siblings; the shorter tower indicated that one had died young. This reading proved to be correct. With the card showing the person, I would ask the spirit world for help, and a thought would pop into my head that the person who had given me the card was waiting for something. The Tarot cards are another way to look beyond the obvious and pick up feelings and information from the spirit world.

As I progressed I found my connection to the spirit world became stronger and stronger. In the circle we gave each other mini readings, either through objects or meditations, which was impressive enough, but Cliff always wanted to push us harder. He would sometimes ask us to do readings blindfolded. When it came to my turn, I would sit in a chair with my eyes covered and everyone in the room shuffled around so I didn't know where anyone was. When the musical chairs stopped, someone would sit down next to me or in the chair behind me and I would have to read them. I would centre myself, plug myself into the resource of energy and start to feel a presence, ask it some questions and go from there. After each piece of information I relayed, they would say yes or no, by nodding or shaking their head, then Cliff would speak the answer so I wouldn't recognize the voice of the person I was reading. This proved to be an invaluable exercise when it came to retrieving as much evidential information as possible.

There were some instances of physical mediumship, too, which were really exciting. Instead of things you can hear and feel in your mind, physical mediumship describes literal ways in which the spirit world interacts with physical objects, or even manifests in a physical form. Unlike meditation, this is a wholly exterior experience, meaning everyone in the room can see what's going on. Some spirits manifest themselves by voice (speaking aloud so that everyone can hear), light and partial or full materialization of body.

From time to time we held séances. This type of group meditation and connection with the spirit world was very popular in the Victorian and early Edwardian era, and it was fashionable in those days to experience everything a séance can provide. People would come away amazed not only by what they had heard from the 'other side' but also by what they had seen. These days, this form of mediumship is exceptionally rare and has very nearly died out. There are a number of reasons for this. Physical mediumship requires intense concentration and it normally takes a long time to get to a level where things start to happen. In today's hundred-miles-an-hour society, people don't have the patience to wait.

We started on a normal Monday evening. We had meditated and were chatting about our experiences to each other when we heard a whistling noise in the room. We looked around to see where it had come from, but couldn't figure it out. It was odd to hear any sort of noise during our meditations because we were all so still and quiet. We shrugged it off – perhaps it had been a faulty boiler – and continued to meditate, sharing our connections and experiences. But after each meditation we heard the whistling again. And again. Meditation and the whistling seemed to go hand in hand. It was as if our combined energy triggered the noise, but we couldn't figure out for the life of us where it was coming from.

The only thing we could see that might have been producing the noise was a cone-shaped object that Cliff had placed on the floor near to our chairs. As the meditation came to a close, the whistling slowly ceased. But we were starting to get excited. Could this be the kind of physical mediumship I'd heard so much about but hadn't yet experienced? We were looking at the cone-shaped object and smiling. The noise was definitely coming from it.

We needed to find out what was going on and what this mundane-looking object was. Cliff explained that it was a spirit trumpet. We looked at each other quizzically. A spirit trumpet? Yes, said Cliff. A spirit trumpet was often placed on a table during séances so that the spirits could make contact through it. It resembled a dunce's cap. Sometimes, Cliff continued, spirits would levitate the trumpet or even condense their energy and pass through it to form a kind of voice box. We were still a bit shocked. So, this object would be used by spirits to ... talk? Yes, Cliff said.

We were nearing the end of the session, so he promised us that the following week, after our meditations, we would explore the spirit trumpet some more.

There was an air of excitement when we gathered together that next Monday night and, sure enough, it wasn't long before Cliff took the trumpet off the floor and placed it on the table. Cliff explained that he had acquired it from a friend and had been told that a dim red light in the room might help it work. The red light was needed, Cliff told us, because bright artificial light or sunlight can be detrimental to any effects or manifestations of physical mediumship: it can degrade the way in which a spirit comes through in any physical form, rather as it would with undeveloped photographic film.

Cliff continued to explain the ins and outs of what we might experience, and told us that if this did work, the spirit would use a visible substance called ectoplasm to manifest. We were all excited and intrigued. We'd only heard a whistling sound from the trumpet up to that point, which was unusual enough, but now we were being told that we would actually see things coming out of it. The only time I had heard of ectoplasm before was in the *Ghostbusters* films, and I associated it with the 'slime' in the movie.

I said this to the circle and everyone chuckled. It's not slime, Cliff told me, and nothing like the movies. Ectoplasm, he said, is an energy form created by the spirit, a bit like plasma. Apparently it was white, and could, on some occasions, bind together to form a whole materialized spirit. Cliff told us that if we wanted a spirit to come through like this, it would take huge effort and concentration on our part to create enough energy for it to appear. If enough ectoplasm was created from the energy of a group, a spirit would pick up on it. Cliff told us that a spirit manifests through ectoplasm as if it is putting on a cloak — it moulds into it so that it becomes a temporary physical body.

Up to this point we had only been in contact with spirits through our minds, thanks to thoughts, feelings, images or sounds. Now we were being told that if we concentrated hard enough and created enough energy in the room, we might see a spirit in front of our very eyes.

That was all the encouragement we needed and we meditated as we had never meditated before. We were determined to make it happen!

We sat around the table in the dim red light. We could just about see each other's faces, but the red light seemed to increase the contrast in everyone's features. It was soft and glowing, but it gave a harsh quality to anything it touched. The trumpet was lying in the middle of the table on its side, the hole at its narrow end facing directly towards me.

We linked our hands, closed our eyes, and went into a deep meditative state, trying to send strong intentions up to the spirit world and building energy in the room. And it was beginning to work. Some people said that, clairvoyantly (through images in their minds), they could see different colours emerging and floating around the trumpet. I didn't pay too much attention to that because I was keeping my eyes tightly closed, trying to create as much energy as possible.

Sue suggested that everyone should channel all their energy to me. Hold on, I thought. What do I do with it when I get it? Cliff calmed me down and explained that, through thought, other members of the circle would send their energy to me, and I, in turn, would send this big block of energy to the trumpet. Use thoughts, Cliff told me. Imagine being filled with all the energy in the room until you're ready to burst. Concentrate on the trumpet. In your mind send the energy to the trumpet. Use thought. Each thought and intention has an energy and vibration unique to itself. Think that you're sending all that energy into the trumpet. Think about all the energy you're receiving and think it all into that trumpet. Put the thought out that you are transferring energy and you will transfer energy.

As Cliff's words continued to guide me, I felt the energy growing inside me. It was similar to when I felt the presence of a spirit in one of my meditations. I felt it inside me, and I felt that presence – the energy

– strengthening. I was concentrating hard, sending the thoughts out to the trumpet. I wanted the spirit world to feel they could use the energy we had provided to take a physical shape. I was thinking about sending all the energy in the room into the trumpet, and at the same time asking the spirit world to make full use of it.

I heard someone gasp. I opened my eyes and saw that wisps of smoke were snaking out of the larger hole pointing away from me. The smoke started to grow a little, build a little, thicken a little. Cliff whispered that this was ectoplasm beginning to form. As it thickened even more, everyone's eyes were wide open. We realized that the smoke had turned into a mist and it was hovering about two feet off the table, but instead of jumping for joy we were deadly silent. We were trying desperately to hold the tension and the energy in the room. All we dared do was glance sideways at each other as if to say a silent WOW! and to acknowledge that we were all seeing the same thing. The ectoplasm was still hovering above the table, and for around six minutes we were transfixed by what, for all of us except Cliff and Sue, was the first time we'd seen any evidence of physical mediumship.

Now it was here, we wanted more. We were willing it to take a more solid form, something more human in shape. We were putting the thoughts out there, but the mist started to deteriorate. It just faded away before our eyes, and soon our experiment with the spirit trumpet was over. We exhaled deeply as Cliff turned off the red light and switched on the normal one. Some rubbed their eyes, others looked reflective or surprised by what they had seen. Even though we hadn't seen the ectoplasm take on human form we weren't disappointed. We had witnessed our first instance of physical mediumship as a group, all thanks to a funny little cone-shaped object.

Nain's Return

Things at the Monday-night circle in Cliff's converted garage were progressing, but that only accounted for a few hours a week. Outside the meetings, my life went on pretty much as normal. I was still going to school – surviving it, hating it – but my alternative education was giving me more of a buzz than the conventional sort.

And I seemed to be catching on quick. With the exercises and techniques I was learning, everything was falling into place. I was able to tap into psychic energy rapidly, and as time went by I was not only able to sit in the energy, but feel it course through me and strengthen my connection to it. This meant I was making some sort of contact with the spirit world every time I meditated. I was gaining confidence, increasingly able to connect with and get evidential information from the spirits who stepped forward. It wasn't long before I was giving readings to other members of the circle and, when I had exhausted all spiritual connection to them, Cliff roped in some of his friends from outside the group.

Monday nights became reading nights, and I would happily sit there, meditate and give readings to Cliff's friends; people I had never met before. A medium is judged on how evidential and accurate the information he or she can relay from the spirit world is, so Cliff was always pushing me to get better information and work on making the images, feelings and sounds given to me by the spirits more vivid and crystal clear.

But I was still new to all this, and whenever I experienced a presence I still felt a sense of wonder and excitement. At first, I wasn't sure what or who these presences in my mind were. But I was learning quickly how to turn their mere being into an almost tangible connection. I looked forward to Monday nights at Cliff's because I felt as if I was going on a journey and being some sort of detective – not only to find out about myself and where I could go to next, but also about other people, in this world and the next.

The Monday nights continued, the readings continued and my development continued, but there was a real world out there away from the circle. On one winter's night the two collided. It was what Mum had been waiting for.

A woman called Gina lived across the road from us. She was a reiki master and had known me since childhood. She was always saying hello, asking me how I was doing at school and how the family was. In Japanese, reiki means universal life energy, and teaches that an unseen energy flows through us. If our life-force energy is low, a reiki healer will gently lay their hands over parts of a patient's body, transferring healing energy.

So you can see why Gina and I hit it off: we both dealt in disciplines and practices that required us to work with energy. Thanks to her friendship with Mum and Nain, whom she had also known well, Gina was one of the few people who knew about my involvement with Cliff's circle and she was always encouraging, asking me how it was going. I didn't talk about my extra-curricular activities at school – I couldn't see the point. I wasn't embarrassed by it, but it was so early in my development that there was no benefit in discussing it with anyone. In any case, can you imagine how my fellow pupils would have reacted? They would probably have teased me something rotten.

Just one person knew, a friend of mine whose mum went to Shirley Spiritualist Church and had seen me come and go there. She must have said to her son, 'You know your friend Ross? Well, you'll never guess where I saw him last night …' But he was genuinely interested in it. He never asked much about it, but when he did he didn't mock me.

And so it was with Gina. Because we shared a common interest in spirituality I often used to pop in for a chat about what she did. I was full of questions and she would answer them in her usual giving, friendly way. It soon got to the stage that whenever I went round she would ask me about my development. I explained to her that meditation was key to how I was progressing, and soon enough I began meditating while Gina was using her reiki healing on me. I was able to 'let go' – completely clear my mind and focus, blocking out all the thoughts that swirl in our minds during our daily lives. This was the only time, other than in the circle, where I learnt on a spiritual level, and meditating with Gina was helpful.

At the end of a meditation, Gina would ask me what I had felt. I had always identified a presence, a familiar one. I was used to feeling these things during the meditations in Cliff's garage, but to feel a presence away from the circle proved to me that this was no fluke. Each time we meditated, the presence got stronger and stronger until I knew which spirit was coming through to me. I couldn't be 100 per cent sure, but it felt like Nain. My beloved grandmother, who had passed only six months or so before, felt close to me. I felt her with me every time I meditated at Gina's.

My mother would often come with me to Gina's and when she saw it was possible that her mum was coming through she couldn't wait to contact her. Let's not forget that I started going to spiritualist churches because my mum was so eager to contact Nain, but my development had almost shunted that goal to one side. Life had simply continued for Mum but now, once again, we had a chance to contact Nain.

One evening we went round to Gina's and I started meditating, while Gina began her healing process. When I was relaxed, the familiar presence appeared. But this time we would try to find out whether it was indeed Nain stepping forward.

Concentrating hard on the presence in my mind, I could almost feel her character traits in me. Her kindness, her willingness to help other people, and that very personal, almost indescribable sensation I'd had whenever I was in her company. I was sure it was Nain, and then something happened that confirmed it: an image of her appeared in my mind. The smiling face, the long blonde hair, the cobalt-blue eyes. It was unmistakably her.

I relayed all this information to Gina and Mum, and even though I had my eyes closed and was focusing hard, I knew that Mum was excited and emotional. Gina began to ask questions.

'What would you like to say, Mair?'

Hearing the question, I asked the presence the same thing. Almost immediately I heard an answer in my mind.

'I just want you all to know that I'm okay, and I'm always around you. Always around …' Nain's reply came through as a thought.

'Ross, can she say anything more, something specific, so we know she's there?' Gina asked.

I frowned. I knew so much about Nain I didn't know what to ask that was so specific and personal it would help to confirm her presence. I ummed and aahed, but Mum, seeing I was struggling to think of anything to ask her, chipped in: 'Ross, before Nain passed she told me something. Something only she and I would know. We were the only two people who discussed it. She wanted to get something for me and your uncle Gwyn. Something I'd remember her by. Ask her what those gifts were.'

Jeez! I thought. I was still unsure how to ask a presence questions in my mind because it was still quite early in my development. But I tried to think about how I had done it before and relaxed, breathed deeply, put the question into my mind, and imagined relaying it to Nain. I thought about the question. I breathed. I asked the question again. What was it you wanted to give to Mum and Uncle Gwyn, Nain? What were the gifts you intended for them? Can you show me or tell me these things?

I repeated the questions and concentrated hard. This was a big deal: it wasn't some random spirit that had stepped forward, it was Nain. If not for me, I wanted to get this information for my mum. It would mean so much to her. Soon enough an image of a gold ring and a gold watch appeared in my mind as clear as I had ever seen. Nothing flash. It was a plain gold ring and a regular gold watch. But a ring and a watch they most definitely were. And I had a feeling coming through attached to each object.

I cleared my throat, aware that my answer was awaited with bated breath. 'Was it a ring for you and a watch for Uncle Gwyn?'

There was silence. I was wondering why someone would want a ring or a watch as a gift: I'd want a new computer games console or something like that. But as I was thinking this, my mum said: 'Yes, it was. It was a ring and a watch that Nain told me she was going to give us.'

That conversation had taken place between my mum and Nain, and neither of them had mentioned it to me, let alone the things she was intending to leave Mum and my uncle. It was a breakthrough, and confirmed that the presence I had felt was indeed Nain. Not only that, but I had managed to retrieve some evidential information. According to Cliff, this was the mark of a good medium and I experienced a rush of emotions: pride, happiness and an indescribable sadness.

Some weeks before I had been in my grandparents' house, and in the bedroom I had shared with Nain. It was late at night and I was sitting on the edge of the bed when I was overcome by a strong sense of despair. I was suddenly distraught and very upset, and I felt this urge to be around people, to hear them and talk to them. But every time I tried to speak I felt that no one would hear me. It was like a waking nightmare. I felt trapped, anxious. I didn't understand the sudden rush of negative emotion and desperation, and I had to steady myself. I had never felt those things before, but there I was, sitting on the edge of the bed in Nain's room and feeling all this horrible stuff. Where was it coming from? What did it mean? It passed soon enough but the desperation was so intense I thought it would never end.

It happened again a few nights later when I was watching telly. I was sitting there, feeling fine, and then WHAM! Those feelings enveloped me again. I wanted to talk to people so much but no one would listen to me. I told Gina about it the next time I saw her and she suggested that perhaps I was picking up something from Nain. Knowing her as she had, Gina said she could imagine her having feelings like that – of trying desperately to reach out to me and my mum, touch us and hug us, but being unable to. I told Mum about it, too, and that was when we had decided to have a real go at contacting Nain.

We were sitting in Gina's house and we had just made contact with Nain. She had told us about the ring and the watch and, more importantly, that she was fine and that she would always be there, looking out for and after us.

'Well, that was quite something.' Gina chuckled, after Nain had gone and I had opened my eyes. 'It was just so lovely that you could get her through, especially since it's been a long time since she passed.'

Now I was back in the room, I couldn't help but agree. We'd been through so much as a family in the past year or so and that evening's events had brought so much relief and peace to us. I looked at my mum. She was still lost in the moment, her eyes misty. But she was smiling at me. This very personal experience proved a point to me, too, but for different reasons. I had just contacted my beloved Nain. That was the moment when I knew that I must carry on my sessions with Cliff. If I could bring joy, relief and peace to people, what else could I achieve?

Psychic Development

Things were happening so fast.
I was changing as a person, and evolving. I had just
turned fifteen and Cliff's teachings were having a serious
effect on me: I was able to get into a meditative state
quickly; I was able to tap into psychic energy and hold
myself within it; I was able to put out intentions and
affirmations; I was able to transfer energy and identify
spirits that stepped forward. Crucially, though, I was also
able to get evidential information from them. The rest
of the circle were always encouraging and supportive.
It was that kind of group. No one looked down on any
other member, and everyone did what they could to
help everyone along.

In many respects I was a typical teenager, feeling
the restlessness of youth in so many parts of my life, but
Cliff's circle provided an oasis of calm in an otherwise
hectic life. Monday night's psychic circle was the
highlight of my week. I looked forward to going into a
meditation and finding out what or who I was going to
meet next.

Cliff had sometimes told me how proud of me he was, and on top of the teachings and words of wisdom, he'd always told me that he was going to push me as hard as he could to further my development, that he was going to do his best to unlock my full abilities. I was chuffed to say the least – someone I respected was taking an interest and believed in me.

One Monday night he pulled me to one side and told me he had arranged two special evenings for me. Both would be at his house and both would require me to give readings for groups of ten people I had never met before. In some ways it was a natural progression from what I was already doing. I had given readings for people in the circle, as well as the odd person Cliff had brought along. But this was at a whole different level. I was excited but very nervous at the prospect. I was still shy, and the idea of standing up in front of all those strangers made me recoil. Cliff told me he would be there, and so would Mum, and I knew I had to give it a shot. He believed in me that much. I couldn't let him down now.

Mum had asked Cliff if he was sure I was ready to take such a big step, but he assured her that I was and she wasn't to worry because I would be looked after. All I knew was that on the day of the reading I was in a different world. That day at school was the longest ever. Time seemed to go so slowly, and as the minutes ticked by I just wanted to get on with it. My nerves were building and all I could think about was doing a good job, not forgetting the techniques I had learnt that had brought me this far and making sure I helped the people who came along.

Until that moment I had never been under pressure. I had coasted through life, especially at school, and had a 'go with the flow' outlook. That Monday night was different. I had to take a deep breath and step up to the plate.

Finally the evening arrived and I found myself in Cliff's converted garage, preparing myself for the main event. In the living room there was an assortment of Cliff's friends from the spiritualist movement. I was pacing up and down in the garage, but I knew that wasn't the right kind of preparation. I needed to relax but I couldn't keep still. Cliff was with me, giving me some last-minute reminders.

'How are you feeling, Ross? All okay? Ready to go?' he asked.

'I think so,' I answered tentatively.

'Just remember a few things. Relax and do what you've always done. But don't ask them any questions. Say, "Can you understand this?" or make statements like, "There is a person here called such-and-such." Don't imply, don't ask. If you're bringing a dad through and you're not sure of his name, don't ask, "What was your dad's name?" If you have a man called Fred, step forward, don't ask, "So who was this Fred to you?" Make statements, don't ask questions. And keep your eyes open.'

He smiled at me.

'You're going to be fine. Now sit and meditate and get yourself ready.'

Cliff was right. I knew I had to get meditating and open myself up to the energies that had served me so well until that point. I sat down, closed my eyes and began to do to what I had done dozens of times before. I made sure I put out some extra special intentions, asked the questions and started to breathe deeply until I felt myself enter my meditative state. I was ready to go to work.

I walked into the room feeling quite relaxed, but wasn't prepared for the sight that greeted me: ten people looking expectantly at me. It was a real deer-in-the-headlights moment. But I knew I just had to do what I had done before. Cliff was sitting in a chair next to me, so I only had to look at him for support if I needed it. But, nerves or no nerves, as soon as I centred myself I became aware of a presence. Today the rest of that reading is a blur. I was on a rollercoaster of adrenalin and calm, giving message after message to the people before me.

I started with a woman sitting on the sofa, and gave her the names of two people who had passed and were stepping forward. She understood them to be family members. One of the women in spirit gave me images and feelings of where she had lived, and showed me herself going for walks in the forest with her mother and playing Pooh Sticks on the river as a child. The woman recognized her mother. I went through every person in the room and starting getting things for them.

Someone's relative had stepped forward and described themselves as an alcoholic; another person's family member described how he was connected to Ireland and was upset when he passed over because he hadn't said some of the things he had wanted to say to his loved ones before he'd left them.

By the end of the evening I was feeling more confident and, more importantly, all the messages I was giving were being taken and validated, and the audience was animated. I was doing my job and, I hoped, doing it well. Every now and then if I asked something that was even remotely like a question, Cliff gave me a little kick and a stern glance: 'Remember, no questions!'

Because I was so young I sometimes found it hard to word things properly, but the contact side of things went much better than I had hoped. My connection to spirit was strong and I had no problem in identifying those who came forward.

When the room emptied and just Cliff, Sue and I were left, they were smiling at me and I breathed a huge sigh of relief. My first public reading. Phew!

'Well done,' Cliff said. 'The next step is for you to do a reading in a church. We start again next Monday night, practising and doing more exercises.'

Ever the straight-talker, Cliff had already planned my next test. I was buzzing after that first reading and the adrenalin was rushing around my body as never before. It took me ages to get to sleep that night.

As promised, it was back to normal the next Monday night in Cliff's garage. More meditations, and more exercises. True to his word, Cliff had indeed arranged with a local spiritualist church for me to do a demonstration. It was time to step up again.

Swaythling is a suburb of Southampton. I had never been there before but there I was, with Cliff, Sue and my mum, driving out of the city and into the 'burbs to give my first public reading in a church. Sue was always there to support me (and continues to be to this day), and she was a very calming, mellow influence, especially on Cliff, who could be quite demanding.

We soon got to the church and went straight into the little room at the back to prepare. It was small, with brown walls and a blue carpet. This was where I would meditate and get ready to face the crowd. I had dressed up for the occasion in my suit, which I had only ever worn at Nain's funeral, an Yves Saint Laurent sleeveless shirt and a clean pair of shoes. I was the smartest I had ever been!

The deal was that Cliff would read from a book about the Second World War and how times had changed since, give an address, and then it was me. For forty minutes! In that back room my heart was pounding. Forty minutes! Were they sure? At that moment forty minutes seemed such a long time. How would I fill it? What would happen if I couldn't contact anyone? If I screwed up? As ever, Cliff was helping me to calm down and get ready. He was telling me to go out there and do my best. To send my thoughts out to the spirit world and meditate. To remember everything we had gone through.

The church president knocked on the door. 'Ready when you are,' he said.

Cliff and I walked through the door and I saw around thirty-five people sitting in front of me. It was more than double the number I had ever read for before and it took me a while to get used to the situation. But as Cliff gave his reading and address, I sat at the side of the stage and put out thoughts and intentions. Please help me make as strong a connection to the spirit world as possible. Please help me to give evidential information. I told myself to do what I'd always done in this situation and trust in spirit, trust that messages would come through.

Before I knew what was happening, the president was introducing me to the crowd. It was my turn to address them, my turn to demonstrate. My heart was pounding and my palms were sweating. But there was no going back now. I stood up on the platform and centred myself. I poured a glass of water and had a shaky sip, closed my eyes and took a deep breath. I opened my eyes and scanned the room. I felt the presence of two people in spirit stepping forward, and through the thoughts, images and sounds I was getting, I was being drawn to a man seated in the back row.

'Sir,' I said, 'I have a gentleman here who says he passed with a heart condition.'

'Okay,' the man said, looking a bit shocked. I closed my eyes again, and more details emerged about one of the men who had stepped forward.

'I've got the name Albert,' I said, remembering what Cliff had told me about not asking questions. 'I feel this was the gentleman who passed with a heart condition.'

'Yes,' the man said again, quietly.

'And I have a second gentleman who's making himself known to me. He's saying his name is Alfred.'

'That was my father.'

I was away. I had identified two men who were related to the man in the back row and, slowly but surely, he was responding. That gave me all the confidence I needed and a flurry of evidential information came through. Alfred was telling me he'd had a problem with his leg before he passed. The man in the back row understood everything. Alfred was his father and Albert his grandfather; they wanted to make themselves known and let their son and grandson know that they were still around in spirit. Still part of his life.

I went to a woman and a man nearer to the front, and brought through a woman I felt had passed, again, from a heart problem. She wanted to talk about someone called Peter, who had a connection with the family: she was worried about Peter's life and the direction he was going in. Again, everything was understood. I was in the flow now, and next I went to a woman in the front row and brought through a woman I felt had passed with

stomach cancer. I started to talk about her personality
and that she was quite an outgoing character. All
understood and validated.

Time was flying by and, before I knew it, it was time
for the last reading of the night. I was drawn to a woman
six rows back, and someone, a woman, had come through
and explained that she had passed with Alzheimer's. The
woman in the audience explained that it was her aunt.
The woman in spirit wanted to let her niece know that she
was watching over her son because he was in the middle
of taking exams.

When the end of the demonstration came I received a
round of applause and felt an enormous rush. Everything
Nain and the mediums at Shirley had said was coming
true. I was on a stage, giving messages to dozens of
people. I had been nervous, yes, but somehow I had got
into a rhythm and gone from one person to the next,
relaying evidential information from the get-go. I was
doing everything Cliff had taught me.

I took a deep breath and looked down. I was
holding on tightly to the back of a chair and swaying
unconsciously. I chuckled to myself – I must have
looked a right idiot! – as people filed out of the church.
Cliff, Sue and Mum were in the third row. Cliff and Sue
were smiling but Mum was crying and smiling at the
same time! She explained afterwards that she'd been
overwhelmed by the combined feelings of nervousness
at the prospect of her son's first church reading and pride

for what I'd achieved. Cliff gave me a pat on the shoulder and we all went home happy.

When Mum and I got back, my dad, brothers and grandfather had put up a 'Well Done' banner outside the front door.

I was living two separate lives. Not much had changed at school but things were moving fast for me in the spiritualist world. I was continuing with the Monday-night circles and doing more readings too. I'd travelled to Winchester with Cliff and Sue to a church there, which had been a success. Everything was coming through crystal clear and I was building confidence as I gave readings in front of larger groups. I was less nervous with each appearance.

I had been in Cliff's circle for around ten months, and felt unstoppable. I was enjoying my journey. It was all happening so fast but I seemed to be taking everything in my stride and adapting to every situation Cliff could throw at me. But then, a bombshell.

Life has a habit of pulling the rug from underneath your feet. I had experienced that crushing reality when Nain got ill and passed so quickly. I was about to experience the same thing.

One day Mum sat me down and told me that Cliff, my mentor, my teacher and friend, had been diagnosed with cancer. Immediately I remembered the black spot on the flower he had brought to the group. He had assured me then that his previous battle with the disease had been successful, so I couldn't believe what Mum was telling me now. The cancer had returned, even more aggressively than before. I didn't know what to say. All the feelings from Nain's last days hit me and I wanted to do something to help Cliff but knew I couldn't do anything. I was, once again, helpless. I was angry at the cruelty of it all and wanted to scream. Why was this happening again, to another person I loved and respected?

Of course, there are no answers in that terrible situation and there is no one to blame.

Life passed in a blur. Naturally the circles at Cliff's house were put on hold while he had treatment. He had stomach cancer, which brought back even more memories of Nain's last weeks. And because I had watched her deteriorate so quickly, I knew that Cliff probably didn't have long left. His actions seemed to bear this out. I heard through friends that he was getting his business in order, tying up loose ends and talking to his family and closest friends, letting them know how he felt. It was almost as if he was preparing to die and saying goodbye.

My limbo state continued. On a selfish level I missed the circle and the new challenges I'd been undertaking, but on another I was thinking about Cliff a lot, hoping he would get better. A few weeks went by and I finally got the call. Cliff wanted to see me and asked if Mum and I could come over to the house. I was dreading it but at the same time I was desperate to see him.

When we got there Sue opened the door. She looked tired, and as we walked into the living room, I got flashbacks from when I'd been visiting Nain in hospital. I felt the same apprehension and dread of seeing someone I loved so poorly. It's one of the most distressing things about terminal illness: the moment you realize that the people whom you thought indestructible are just as susceptible to illness as anyone else.

And there was Cliff, sitting in his armchair, just as I had remembered Nain. He was pale and gaunt, with a blanket draped over him, a shell of his former self. It was heartbreaking. He was usually smiling and mischievous. Now talking took up all his energy.

We chatted about what the doctors had told him, what he needed to do to sort a few things out, and he even apologized for not being able to help me more. I smiled but I wanted to cry. He believed in me and he was apologizing. As ever he was thinking of other people before himself. As we chatted I soon realized that this was probably the last time I would see him. I thought there and then that I wasn't going to let him down, and that I would become the best medium I could possibly be.

His condition was worsening in front of our very eyes, and our chat was tiring him out. It was time to say goodbye. Before we left, he gave me a piece of paper with a phone number on it and explained that it would put me in contact with friends of his who had agreed to help me when he was no longer around.

'Ring them, Ross,' he said. 'They're good people who will look after you when you do more readings. You need to do more and I want you to really push yourself. I believe in you and I know you can do it. I'm just sorry I'm not going to be able to help any more.'

And with that things got really emotional. He gave my mum a hug and then me. He was crying, Sue was crying, Mum was crying and I was crying. We hugged one last time and he whispered in my ear: 'Don't worry, I'll be helping you from the other side.'

Through my tears, I whispered back unsteadily, 'Thank you – thank you.'

Cliff was taken into hospital just a week later and passed away.

Turning Professional

Cliff had asked me to ring Chris, and I wasn't about to let him down. As president of Southampton Spiritualist Church, Chris was, as I later found out, a well-known figure in spiritualist circles throughout the city. I had arranged to visit him at his house in a quiet suburb, and when the day came I was nervous. Things had been going so well with Cliff, but now tragic circumstances had dictated that I was to have a new friend.

I had seen Chris once before, at Cliff's funeral. It had been held at a spiritualist church in Southampton and Cliff's family and friends (in and outside the spiritualist movement) had gathered to pay tribute to a man who had given so much to so many people. It was amazing to see. Even though we had had a close, special relationship, there were so many people from different walks of life that I realized I had played only a small part in Cliff's. So many people had loved and respected him. Sue was there, of course, and, as you can imagine, she was very emotional. Her son Ian got up to say a few words.

He talked about everything Cliff had been involved with, how much he had helped people and that one person in particular had been the most recent beneficiary of his good work. Ian told the congregation that I was going from strength to strength and had already started to serve churches.

We were both busy at Cliff's funeral – Chris with his administrative role, and me with my emotions – so we didn't have a chance to talk. So, on the day of our first meeting, I was apprehensive. What would he think of me? What if he didn't like the way I did things? What if Chris wasn't happy with what I had learnt from Cliff? Would I be able to get the same results now Cliff wasn't around? All those questions were spinning in my head as Mum drove me to Chris's house.

I needn't have worried. Chris's wife, Gill, greeted me with a warm smile and straight away explained that she had seen me in action at one of the spiritualist churches in the city. During my all-too-brief time with Cliff I had been travelling around Southampton and demonstrating at churches, and she hadn't forgotten me.

'Hello, Ross,' she said. 'The last time I saw you, you were giving a demo and managed to give one of the women in the audience the name of the road where some of her family lived. That was quite something!'

Ah, that one. I remembered speaking with a woman in the audience and giving her some evidential information I had received from one of her relatives who had passed over. It was the first time I had managed to get such pinpoint information from the spirit world and when I'd offered her the name of the road she had nodded, open-mouthed. You can't get more specific than that, I'd thought at the time, and I was relieved that I had managed to uphold one of Cliff's golden rules: make sure you get as evidential as you can, as early as you can. I'd glanced at Cliff after I'd relayed the information, and he had smiled as if to say, 'Well done, Ross. That's the kind of stuff people want and need.'

Now I was talking with Chris in his house. He explained that he had given Cliff some healing during his first battle with cancer a decade earlier, and even though they had been attached to different churches they had struck up a friendship. I could see why. Chris was calm, open and friendly, softly spoken, with a little joke here and a smile there. I soon felt comfortable in his presence.

Chris and Gill were full of compliments, and said they had not only seen me on the circuit but had heard great things about me. We all knew we weren't there to pat each other on the back, though: we were there to figure out what came next for me. Since Cliff had passed I'd been stuck in a bit of a rut. I had been progressing so fast and enjoying every minute of my journey, but without Cliff, the momentum had ground to a halt.

I was desperate for my spiritual development to continue and keen to know how Chris could help.

Cliff had insisted I ring him, but I had no idea what they had said about me or what he could do for me. Seeing my anxiety, Chris calmly explained that before Cliff had passed he had made him promise to look after me. Cliff had explained that I had been developing rapidly but still needed some guidance. I had learnt so much in such a short time that it would be a shame if my development stopped.

I was relieved when I heard this. It was such a huge compliment from someone I admired so much. And I agreed with him – I didn't want to stop! For the first time in my life I knew what I wanted. Everything about it felt right. Cliff's compliments added determination to my ambition. There was no way I was going to let him down, and, thankfully, Chris told me he wanted to help me. He would be happy to arrange bookings at churches, drive me to and from demonstrations and other public events, and generally look after me.

We agreed that we'd take it slowly – it was big commitment for both of us – and if there were any problems between us, we could just walk away, no hard feelings. We knew it would be difficult. We had lost a respected friend, and I was stepping onto a new path. But we also knew we had to try. Chris had promised Cliff to help me where he could, and I was determined not to let Cliff's good work go to waste.

The best way to start, we thought, was to arrange for me to demonstrate at a service as soon as possible.

The first service we did together was at Ringwood Spiritualist Church in Hampshire, a perfect location because it wasn't too far from home. It was my first demo without Cliff but in my meditating time before I went on, I centred myself, put out the sort of intentions Cliff had taught me and got ready to carry on the good work. I was nervous, but everything went according to plan. I connected to the spirit world in the same easy way I had been able to with Cliff at my side, and the evidential information came thick and fast.

That night lifted a weight off my own and Chris's shoulders. I proved to myself that I could connect to the spirit world in a public demonstration without Cliff physically by my side, and Chris knew that I was the real deal.

In the immediate aftermath of Ringwood I started to socialize more with Chris and Gill and slowly built up a friendship with them. They were fairly recently retired, loved cricket and were passionate about the spiritualist movement. They were also great company. We chatted about my development, went out for meals and I started to attend more and more services at churches. They were a steadying influence and let me develop in the way Cliff had intended. They were neither hands-on nor hands-off. We just clicked and started to enjoy our time together.

It seemed that Cliff's plan of action was taking shape. I hadn't lost the ability to connect to the spirit world, and I was starting to get back on track. Chris and Gill were ferrying me from one church to another, offering helpful advice and making sure I stayed on an even keel. I really couldn't have asked for more from them, and with Mum and the rest of my family supporting me, I could attack the circuit and continue my development. Without Cliff guiding me, though, I had to take responsibility for my learning. That was another of his golden rules: always keep learning and be hungry for knowledge.

Well, I wanted to learn and develop: just shy of my sixteenth birthday, I had found something I was good at. I like to think Cliff, as he'd promised when I saw him for the last time, was having a little smile to himself in spirit. And, knowing Cliff, he would have been saying: 'Enough chat! Now let's get to work.'

Before I could do anything, though, it was time to say goodbye to my school. But I needed a plan. My attendance had been poor ever since Nain had passed, while the startling developments in Cliff's circle and then my journeys on the road with Chris and Gill meant that in many ways I had left school mentally a long time before my official leaving date. I swung by to lessons that vaguely interested me, but really to make sure that I wasn't excluded for being absent.

When I was at school I found it difficult to concentrate. So much else was going on in my life that what took place within those walls seemed irrelevant. I was mixing with adults – some of whom were more than three times my age – and actually helping people at their time of grief or spiritual indecision. It was weird. I wasn't even sixteen, yet I was doing such adult and important things that I felt my time at school was wasted. I could be out there doing more of the things I loved, but for now I was stuck.

In many ways, the time I'd spent with Cliff, Chris and Gill, and at the various churches I visited, gave me a new perspective on things at school. Whereas before I was only too happy to mix with the other boys, muck around and play pranks, now I wasn't interested in them. School seemed inconsequential and boring. I had seen people suffer, and I had suffered myself in the past year or so, yet all my schoolmates wanted to do was throw things at each other and deal in contraband chewing gum. The sooner I got out of that place, the better. I knew what I wanted to do, and my mind was made up.

The last few months had shown me that I could explore my spirituality and help people. I had seen that the contact I could make with the spirit world could soothe people's grief, give them evidential information to prove the continuity of life and reassure them that their loved ones were still with them wherever they went. I knew how they felt too. After Nain had passed I'd thought a lot about what happens next, and I often felt anxiety and confusion because our physical form isn't indestructible. But thanks to Cliff's circles and the demonstrations, I had seen what lies ahead. Connecting to the spirit world comforted me too.

So, my mind was set. I wanted to serve the spirit world, and help people. I would become a full-time medium. The only thing I had left to do was break it to my mum and dad.

As my sixteenth birthday approached, Mum and Dad had, quite naturally, been asking what I was going to do next. Had I anything in mind? As time went by they asked me more frequently. Although my parents, especially my mum, had seen how things had been developing with me spiritually, they hadn't the foggiest idea that I was thinking of becoming a professional medium. I had to sit them down and tell them.

It had been six months or so since I had first met Chris and Gill, but during our short time together — and after I had decided to make a real go of becoming a professional medium — I had told them that after I left school I was going to turn professional; I would be doing public events and readings at venues all over the country. They would drive me to and from each engagement, and I would give private readings too.

When I said this to Mum and Dad, the knowledge that I would have supervision calmed Mum a bit, because her own and Dad's initial reaction to what I'd told them was along the lines of 'Well, if you choose that, you've got a hell of a job on.' But, all credit to my parents, they also said that if mediumship made me happy, and I was sure that that was what I wanted to do, they would support me. Of course they were concerned, and they had every right to be. I was sixteen and starting a business. Not only that, but the business I was about to start was pretty unusual. No one had tried it so young before. There were plenty of professional mediums but they were all much older than I was. Much, much older. I would have to work harder than I had ever worked in my life for my venture to succeed.

Once I had decided to become a professional medium, the priority was to make sure it happened. The day after I left school I woke up a free man. I jumped out of bed (unusual for me!) and looked out of the window, thinking, Yes! I don't have to go to school any more! It was as if a huge weight had been lifted off my shoulders. But it was also a bit surreal: I was so used to the routine of getting up, putting on my uniform and going to school. Now I didn't have to do any of that. Unofficially I was a professional medium, and I spent my first day of not being at school basking in my new status.

That lack of activity didn't last long. Driven by the determination to fulfil my ambitions, I filled in various documents to set myself up as a self-employed person and registered my business name: Teen Psychic. The forms asked me what I planned to do for a living, and I wrote 'professional medium'. I looked down and there it was, on paper. It was official. I was a professional medium.

But my new status was just the start. I had some business cards made up, and I did the odd reading, thanks to word of mouth in the local area and to people seeing my cards in a few of the local shops I put them in.

The first reading I did as a professional was a private one for a woman and her family. Sitting in the car beforehand, I was nervous – this was my first professional reading and I wanted so much to do a good job, not only for the clients but also for me. I had given readings before but this felt different. Being the figurehead for your own business means that you live or die by your reputation, and I was determined that my first professional reading would go well.

When I arrived at her house, my client greeted me and showed me into her living room. She was sitting on her sofa and I stood in front of her, moving from side to side, turning around, turning back again, raising my energy to get a strong connection with spirit.

I'd meditated in the car, and when I put out my intentions I'd included some that would help me relax because I was feeling extra pressure. I took deep breaths, as I'd learnt to do in Cliff's circle, and opened my eyes. I had to tell myself to keep doing what I had always done: go to the quiet places in my mind, open myself up, tap into the reservoir of psychic energy and send out as many intentions as I could. If I did that I'd be fine.

'Do you need me to do anything?' the woman asked.

'No, not at all. Just relax and let me do all the work. There's nothing to worry about. I'm ready when you are.' Even though I was nervous, I was trying to put her at ease.

I sank into a comfy chair, breathed deeply again, and immediately felt a presence. Someone had stepped forward. He wasn't saying much – Great, I thought, a quiet one to start things off! – but I asked him some questions gently and, sure enough, he became more expressive, showing and telling me memories of someone I assumed had been very close to him.

'Well,' I said, 'a man has stepped forward. He seems gentle and quiet. He's not saying a lot, but he's trying to show me something …' I paused. 'He's showing me an image of a doll. This doll has a little blue dress on. Can you understand this?'

She looked at me with a sparkle in her eye and smiled. 'Yes … yes, I can …'

Inwardly I was relieved – in my first reading as a professional, my client was accepting the first piece of evidential information I'd given her. That really helped to settle me down. I was now in a confident frame of mind.

'This gentleman is showing me a beach. I can almost hear the waves. He's telling me he used to take you there as a child, and that you used to run along the beach trying to catch the seagulls. He's telling me he always bought you an ice cream at the end of each trip. You loved ice cream …'

'Yes, I did. But I hated getting sand in my swimming costume.' She laughed, her eyes beginning to mist. 'We used to spend ages trying to get the damn sand out. I'd always find more, though!'

And then a name. A name so clear it was like hearing the voices I'd heard in my mind when I was younger. But instead of the voice saying, 'Ross,' it was saying 'Norman'.

'He's telling me his name is Norman. Can you understand that name?'

She broke down in tears. 'Yes,' she said, reaching for a tissue. 'Norman was my dad.'

Once she had calmed down she thanked me, and told me that hearing from her father was a great comfort to her.

But my work there wasn't done. After I had finished her reading, she asked if, while I was there, I could give more. I said, 'Sure,' and into the living room walked her partner and her daughter.

My first professional appointment was quite a test – the entire family wanting a reading in their home – but once I was in my groove there was no stopping me. I had managed to connect strongly with spirit and I was able to help each member of that family by proving to them that their deceased loved ones were still alive in spirit and were still looking out for them. I left that house raring to go.

As time went by, the number of readings I was doing increased. Thanks to the business cards and word of mouth, I saw private clients a few times a week and demonstrated at a church a couple of times a month. And then I was asked to appear on a BBC3 show called *I Believe*. A scouting team had contacted me to ask if they could film one of my demonstrations in Bournemouth, show the result to their boss and decide if I was suitable for the programme. The production people and I had a little chat about what would be required in front of the camera. I learnt pretty quickly that you have to block out the cameras or your connection to the spirit world won't be as clear as it normally would. I had to focus extra hard during that demo – I was excited and a little bit nervous – but I sensed that if I just did what I usually did they would be impressed. Besides, my first obligation was to the people in that church who had turned up to make a connection to their recently passed loved ones. I couldn't let them down, and thankfully I didn't: the readings went well, despite the cameras.

The production team explained that the show they were preparing for was to star Joe Swash of *EastEnders* and *I'm a Celebrity ... Get Me Out of Here*, who came to see me demonstrate while I was filmed. We popped out to a café, where we were filmed chatting more about what I do, how I do it and the spirit world.

That experience definitely gave me a taste for being on television, and made me realize that I could take what I did and spread it to a much bigger audience. The film of me with Joe in Bournemouth was shown on BBC3 and repeated on channels throughout Europe and America. I also appeared on radio in Wales and the Isle of Wight, and gave some newspaper interviews. Things were going pretty well. Even though it was weird being interviewed by journalists, it was invaluable in terms of exposure and getting my name out there. The best thing was that they were coming to me – it seemed my reputation as an up-and-coming young spirit medium was getting around.

Because I was appearing on and in various media, my secret was out. I'd only recently left school and just one of my friends knew about my extra-curricular activities. Now there was no hiding place, but the feedback I got from former fellow pupils was positive. In fact, they were intrigued. They had shared a classroom with me for four or five years and knew me well but had never discovered what had been going on in Cliff's circle. Whenever I bumped into any of them in town, they'd always be supportive and interested in what I did. The usual comment I got was 'You kept that quiet!' and they were right, for good reason. I hadn't wanted anything to interfere with my spiritual development.

One of the my ex-schoolmates went to college and got a degree but couldn't use it because there were no jobs available in his field. Two ex-classmates are working at supermarkets and a third is trying to get an apprenticeship with an electrician. It's tough out there, so I'm always incredibly thankful that I took the plunge when I did. When I look back on my first year as a professional, where I've come from, what I've experienced and some of the amazing places I've travelled to, I still have to pinch myself.

Recently an old classmate got in touch with me on Facebook, which reminded me of an incident at school.

In my last year, this friend, another boy and I were in my bedroom. We used to take turns to go round to each other's houses to hang out and play on our games consoles. That occasion was no different from any other post-school hang-out, and we were chatting when a glowing light appeared in the middle of the room. It emerged from nowhere – a bit like the hand-shaped light I'd seen in my grandparents' house when I was much younger – and put a stop to our conversation.

My friends had seen it too: they were staring in a what-the-hell-is-that? sort of way. I sensed a presence in the room. It was quite a strong one, but I didn't want to ask it any questions because my two worlds had just collided in spectacular fashion. Until then I had kept them separate. During the day I was a teenager going to school and hanging out with my mates, and in the evening (specifically Monday evening at Cliff's place), I was developing my abilities. My friends didn't know this, of course. But there I was in my bedroom and we were all seeing this light. I wasn't sure how to react. If I'd said, 'Don't worry, lads, I'll just have a word with the presence to see what it's all about, who it is and where it's from,' they'd have looked at me a bit funny. No, I couldn't do that. My other life would have been revealed, and I wasn't quite ready for that yet. Instead we gawped at the light until, after about five seconds, it faded away.

I was calm because I had seen much more than a random light at Cliff's circle, but my mates turned to me and asked me what it could have been. I said something along the lines of 'Dunno … Could have been anything.'

'Wow, it was pretty freaky,' one said.

I just smiled and nodded. Little did they know.

After our Facebook conversation my friend and I arranged to go for lunch. When we met in town he smiled and shook my hand. 'You're doing pretty well for yourself as a medium!'

'I've been at it for almost four years,' I replied, wondering how he would respond. It's not every day you meet an old schoolfriend who's gone on to become a medium. You'd expect them to say they were at university or sixth-form college, or working in one of the local shops or factories.

'Good for you, mate. You know, when I sent you that message on Facebook, I remembered that time in the bedroom when the light appeared. I always thought there was something going on with you after that. You took it so calmly, like it wasn't the first time you'd seen something like it. I'm not surprised you've gone into this.'

I was relieved and gratified that he was so open-minded – and his reaction was similar to that of other people who had kept in contact or I'd bumped into. One old schoolmate, who worked in a clothes shop and recognized me while I was shopping recently, said to me: 'I see you're quite famous now!'

'I don't do too bad,' I replied, and we had a nice chat about what I did and the old days.

My secret had been well and truly out for a while now: my two worlds had collided. The good news was that no one was teasing me, and they were more supportive than I could ever have hoped.

And the business was going well. In the year since I had turned professional, I had gone from posting cards in newsagents' windows to receiving phone calls from people all over the country asking for private readings. On top of that I was still being booked by spiritualist churches. It was such a whirlwind that I had no time to step back and reflect. The fears my mum and dad had had about me turning professional were put to bed once and for all (in fact, after my BBC3 appearance, my dad said he was proud and that 'It was great to see you on the old goggle-box, son').

Although it was very early in my career, my recent success had given me a taste for more. It was time to take things to the next level.

Coming of Age

I was sixteen and everything was going pretty well. I was busy helping people from all walks of life, both in private readings and at public events, which made me feel great. I had found my niche, my calling. This was what I was meant to do.

One of the Internet sites I used to visit was a spiritual chatroom, where like-minded people can talk about anything to do with spiritualism and their beliefs. I got talking to an American girl living in Canada, and found that we had quite a lot in common. She told me that some of her family members were psychic at different levels. She was fascinated by what I did and how I did it, and our conversations in the chatroom soon mutated into long chats on Messenger and Skype.

There was one big problem: she lived thousands of miles away in New Brunswick and I was in Southampton. It was a long-distance relationship, which wasn't ideal, but we were growing closer and closer until there was only one thing for it: I had to visit my girlfriend.

We decided it might be good to go on a road trip. After all, it was my first visit to North America, so why not make the most of it? I could arrange some private readings while

I was there – my first on foreign soil, a great challenge. So off I went to Canada. When I met my girlfriend she was even more beautiful in the flesh than she had been in the webcam conversations I'd had with her. I gave some readings in Canada, and then we travelled over the border into America, cruising through Maine, New Hampshire and Massachusetts until we reached New York. The buildings seemed enormous, the city bustling with life and energy, and there were so many things to see and do. While I was there I managed to squeeze in some private readings I had set up before I left England, which all went well. I've always been level-headed and so, even though it was great to be with my girlfriend and in New York, I was always able to centre myself and prepare for readings as I would at home: relax, focus, meditate and make contact. And, of course, find out as much evidential information as I could from those in spirit who stepped forward.

Soon we were ready to drive back to New Brunswick, along the eastern seaboard. Watching my girlfriend and the gorgeous New England scenery as we sped by, I realized I wanted to be with her. We'd had such a great time during the week or so we'd spent together and we knew we had to try to make it work. The distance between our homes made things difficult, but we decided that my girlfriend would visit several times a year. Later, she moved to England and I'm happy to say that we now live together.

It had been a little over a year since I'd turned professional, and by now I was travelling all over the place and being interviewed on radio and in national magazines. I felt full of confidence: I had refined the techniques I had learnt with Cliff into my own set of rituals and had worked on my onstage confidence. Everything was flowing and my connections to the spirit world were becoming easier, helped by my spirit guides.

You've probably heard of spirit guides. A lot of famous mediums have them – a medium's spirit guide can become more famous than the medium! It'll help a psychic connect to the spirit world. A spirit guide is like an intermediary. If a medium is having trouble contacting a spirit or the connection to the spirit world isn't as clear as it might be and the person stepping forward is distant or having trouble communicating, a medium will call on his or her spirit guide to help them achieve a stronger connection and to clarify information. It's almost as if a spirit guide is there to reassure a spirit who's a bit shy when contact is made. Different mediums use spirit guides in slightly different ways, but the common thread is that they're there to help.

Of course, when Mountain Horn had first come through to me I had no idea what a spirit guide was or how he could help me. I was at my first circle in Cliff's garage. We were meditating, as we always did at the start of a session, when I became aware of an impressive man in my mind. He looked Native American in origin and was wearing khaki-coloured clothes and a headdress with horns on it. I was amazed. I hadn't seen anyone like him before, only in books and films. His skin was tanned like leather, and he had hard, staring eyes. He told me his name was Mountain Horn and that he was going to be there for me. Not all the time, but whenever I needed him he'd be in the background.

I was shocked. Until then I had been in contact only with Caucasian people who spoke good English and were content to hang around so that I could relay information about their lives to someone in the circle. But Mountain Horn was different. As with the spirit woman I'd seen when I was a child, I knew that he was not from our time and was pretty sure that he had existed in physical form way before anyone in the circle had been born. Way before. He was old, and his craggy face gave him a wise, intense look that commanded respect. And he wasn't overly keen on sticking around – he said his piece and was gone in the blink of an eye.

After the circle had wrapped up for the evening, I told Cliff what I had seen and he explained that Mountain Horn might be a spirit guide, and that what he had said – that he would be there for me but not all the time – sounded like prime spirit-guide material. People in the spirit world helped him too, he added, so this was nothing out of the ordinary.

Suddenly, out of nowhere, I had my own spirit guide. How could I get hold of him? Was there a special way that I could contact him when I needed him? Could I call on him in everyday situations to help me with everyday decisions? I had to keep coming back to what Mountain Horn had told me: he would always be there, but only if I needed him. He had said it with a serious face, which seemed to suggest that I should heed his words: his 'service' wouldn't be like a tap I could turn on and off as I pleased.

At this stage of my development I was on a voyage of discovery and, with the various exercises Cliff was teaching the circle and experiences like the spirit trumpet, the ways in which I was being able to tap into energy were improving all the time. In many ways I didn't need Mountain Horn. Some mediums use spirit guides almost daily. My connection to Mountain Horn wasn't (and isn't) like that. He would pop up at certain times, but months might pass without my hearing from him. And when he did show up he proved himself to be a man of few words. But he was there. Always there.

I was happy I had a spirit guide. Mountain Horn had come out of the blue, but what happened next took me even more by surprise: another guide contacted me, then another. The second told me his name was Red Moon. Once again, he showed himself to me in a meditation. Like Mountain Horn, he was a man not of this age or time: Red Moon said he was from Ancient Egypt. One of the few subjects that had interested me at school was history, so I knew my Ancient Roman from my Ancient Egyptian clothing, and Red Moon was definitely Egyptian. Where he also differed from Mountain Horn was that he was willing to stay longer to chat, so I could ask him more questions. He told me about the techniques his people had used to construct their buildings, about his position as a priest and how organized religion back then was very different from what we have now.

There were multiple deities who were believed to be in control of elements of nature. Each element had its own god, and there were dozens of them: Tawaret for childbirth, Osiris for the dead, Tefnut for moisture, Khepri for creation and rebirth, Thoth for knowledge, Nut for the sky, and Ra for the sun, to name but a few. Ancient Egyptians paid tribute to all the different aspects of life, things we often take for granted or overlook, so I was excited when Red Moon took an interest in me. His message was similar to the one I had received from Mountain Horn: I want you to know that I'm here; I might not be talking to you all the time, but I'll always be helping you with what you do.

And then he said: 'You have much work ahead of you. There are many people in the spirit world who will be trying to help you and there are many watching your progress.'

Well, I thought, no pressure, then!

When I asked him what this meant, he continued: 'I can't reveal too much at this stage in your development, but more will become apparent as your pathway progresses.'

'Oh, oh … Okay.' I swallowed. So I had an audience in spirit; I immediately wondered who the spirits were and why they were taking such an interest. But just then Cliff called us to attention and it was time to start another exercise. I put thoughts of my spirit guides to the back of my mind and that was where they stayed. I had card readings and spirit trumpets to deal with!

The most recent guide to get in touch was a man called Alexander. Like Mountain Horn and Red Moon, he came to me during a meditation, but unlike them, Alexander – or Alex, as I call him – came to me fairly recently. I first met him in 2011, and he's the one I'm in touch with most often.

When you communicate with a spirit you get an idea of their personality, their sense of humour, or, conversely, their anxieties or quirks. Mountain Horn and Red Moon didn't say much and had an air of quiet confidence. I felt a sternness about them, too, which gave them authority. Alex had all these qualities, but he was much more talkative. Serious, yes, but there was an element of mischief to him, which made him more approachable. Wise, but funny. That's the best way I can describe Alex. He tends to help me when someone from the spirit world is shy in coming forward or if the contact isn't as strong as it should be, and when he's asking them questions on my behalf I can hear and feel that he has a nice friendly way.

When we first made contact, Alex told me about his origins. Whenever anybody mentions the name Alexander I automatically think of Alexander the Great –

the Macedonian warrior king who was tutored by Aristotle and conquered Persia more than three hundred years before the birth of Christ. But even though my Alexander told me he came from the same sort of era, he was at pains to make clear he was definitely not *the* Alexander. My Alexander, from the words, feelings and images he has shown me during the months I've known him, was alive in physical form several centuries after Alexander the Great, but he did have some connections with the great man. Such was Alexander the Great's impact on Ancient Greece, and specifically Macedonia, that my Alexander was named after the fêted king and lived in Pella, the ancient capital of Macedonia and the city where Alexander the Great had been born. Alex also told me that when he was alive in physical form he had been a very wise man, had a seat on the senate of the city council and was a diplomat.

I could've sat listening and chatting to him all day when we first met. He was so interesting and friendly. And quite cheeky too – he was always making little jokes at my expense or making fun of a situation. You'll see what I mean a bit later on.

So, now I had three spirit guides, all from noble ancient cultures. I couldn't have picked better. You could have a big debate on the importance of spirit guides to a medium, but they don't bother me too much. It's a comfort to know that they're in the background during public demonstrations, giving me energy and helping everything come together. A spirit guide's main job is to make sure the energy flows. They help give me energy to connect to the spirit world, and they give the spirits who step forward a boost too. They're like intermediaries, conduits and go-betweens in one. The role Alex carried out when he was alive in physical form – a diplomat – was the perfect training for a spirit guide. No wonder he's so effective.

I won't call upon them on an everyday basis. I simply call them during meditations, and when I put out my intentions, I always make sure I include some messages for my spirit guides, asking them for help in making the best possible connection. Something like 'I need your help. Please help me to make the best possible connection to the spirit world. Make it strong and clear and help me contact those spirits who want to step forward in the best way possible.' They don't necessarily acknowledge me but, as they have told me, they're always there.

One specific instance of how my guides have helped me happened a year or so ago. I was giving a private reading to a woman and I made contact with a younger man. During our conversations, he was bringing through lots of different emotions, and showing me memories and connections from when he was alive in physical form. He showed me how he passed, and told me that his was a very sudden and unexpected passing. No one knew that he was ill and when he collapsed it was a shock to everyone. There was never a satisfactory medical explanation, and to this day his family and friends are unsure what happened to him.

The woman took all this information and confirmed it to be true, and explained that the man who had stepped forward was an ex-lover of hers. She explained, a little sheepishly, that she had been having an affair with him when he had passed so suddenly, and that she had been planning to leave her now ex-boyfriend for him.

As a medium, I often share very personal moments and information with the person I'm giving a reading to and the spirit who has stepped forward. Such situations can get very emotional, but I never judge people on how they live their lives or what they've got up to. I'm always more interested and focused on making sure the connection to the spirit world is as pure as it can be so that I can gather and convey as much evidential information as possible.

That was the case with this woman and her ex-lover, who had passed and with whom I was now communicating in the spirit world. I wasn't about to judge them for having had an affair: I just wanted to give her as much information as I could. And the information was flowing. I felt that they had worked together in a restaurant and he was showing me a connection to a pub. That was where they'd met, he told me, and had got to know each other. Because they were working together they had spent a lot of time with each other, so their friendship had blossomed into something more. He talked about them going for drives in his car – he was a bit of a boy racer type – and he brought through the names of family and friends they would both know.

It was all making sense to the woman, and she was nodding and smiling at every piece of information I brought through.

I hit a brick wall when it came to the man's name. Everything had been coming through so clearly, but I just couldn't get his name. Couldn't hear it, couldn't see it and couldn't feel it. I tried asking him but there was nothing. Everything ground to a halt and the connection went quiet. I was determined to find out his name, not least for my own curiosity, but for my client as well. Even though she was confirming all the information I was bringing through to her, she needed a name to confirm that the spirit who had stepped forward was who she thought he was.

And then I remembered my spirit guides. They'd always told me that they would be there when I needed them. It's very rare that I use them during a reading but this was different. I asked for a guide to help me. On this occasion Alex came through – he was always the loudest and most frequent presence when it came to my guides. I said in my mind: 'Alex, could you show me somebody I know who shares this guy's first name?'

Sure enough, a moment later I got an image that took me by surprise but helped me to identify the man's name. I was shown an image of a guy I had given a reading to and had kept in touch with ever since through Facebook. I remembered he was young and had never been for a reading before because he was sceptical about the process. I managed to bring his grandfather through, which had changed his opinion of the spirit world and mediums. This was the person I saw in my mind after I had asked Alex to help me. His name was Stuart and so, without hesitation, I asked if she could understand that name.

When she heard it she burst into tears and said: 'Yes, that's his name. The person you've been talking about for the last half hour is Stuart. Thank you.'

Silently I passed on my thanks to Alex.

Once, my guides stepped in to help me in a way that perhaps goes against the grain. I understood that they wouldn't usually intervene in my life, but they're true to their word – always around but never showing themselves unless they absolutely have to.

Before I'd met my girlfriend, I'd been seeing an older woman, which hadn't gone down too well with some members of my family. She was a lovely person, but they were naturally worried and wondered if it was the right relationship for me. I was playing outside in the back garden with my little brother Todd when Red Moon suddenly appeared in my mind. Like Mountain Horn, he is the strong, silent type and only appears very occasionally. He said: 'A person is going through your phone.'

That stopped me in my tracks. It was quite a random thing to get an unasked-for message from Red Moon, but to hear a person from Ancient Egypt talk about a modern mobile phone was unusual to say the least. So I popped my head around the corner so I could see through the kitchen window and, sure enough, a member of my family was holding my mobile and going through my messages. It was obvious what they were doing: they were checking up on me and seeing whether there was anything incriminating to support their view that my then-girlfriend was bad news. I ran into the kitchen – yes, I actually ran – to catch them in the act.

When I got to there, I blurted out: 'What are you doing?'

Talk about being caught red-handed! They just stood there, mouth open, holding the phone, then came up with some excuse about the phone going off and it wouldn't stop ringing so they'd picked it up and tried to turn it off. I smiled and said: 'Yeah, of course. Thanks for picking it up for me.'

The incident made me laugh, but Red Moon had intervened in a way I hadn't experienced before. Maybe Mountain Horn, Red Moon and Alex were right: whatever the situation, big, small or slightly random, they would be looking out for me.

When I tell people about my spirit guides it sounds like the start of a joke: a Native American, an Ancient Egyptian and a Macedonian walked into a bar … They're anything but. Because of their amazing histories, cultures and wisdom, I've got a huge amount of respect for them, and value their help when I lose my connection to the spirit world or it isn't quite as strong as it might be. They do a brilliant job, and I couldn't do what I do without them.

On the Road

Ever since I turned professional my life has been a bit of a whirl, but I soon learnt that being a medium on the road is less than glamorous. During the last four years I've travelled up and down the country, appearing at public events all over Britain and in every part of the south of England.

There have been a lot of early starts, hours on motorways and late nights. I always like to have half an hour before any demonstration to meditate, but sometimes, thanks to terrible traffic and adventures along the way, I've more or less had to walk straight from the back seat of a car and into an event to perform. I have to be ready for anything, and it's been an amazing journey so far, but the travelling and the logistics of getting from one place to another are only the half of it. I've met some amazing people, shared some incredible experiences and strengthened my connection to the spirit world in ways I could never have imagined.

The people I meet react in different ways to readings (and in different ways to a tattooed youngster giving them), but they have all been positive. Some have been incredibly moving, while others have been funny and inspirational. And there are great stories that I've mentally stockpiled, which I'd like to share with you now.

A couple of years ago I hosted a Hallowe'en event in Havant. I was being drawn to a bald-headed chap sitting impassively a few rows behind the woman to whom I'd been giving a reading. He looked serious – and quite tough. I told him I had a man coming through for him and asked if it was all right for me to talk to him.

'Yeah, yeah, sure.' He shrugged.

'I'm getting the name James from this man.'

'He was my uncle,' he replied.

'I'm also getting the feeling that in life he had the impression that certain people in the family didn't really like him and tried to avoid him. And I'm getting a strong feeling that he liked to keep some things about his life secretive, even from his family. He's telling me that people were nervous around him, that they didn't like to be with him.'

'You're right. James was a gangster in Glasgow so we always gave him a wide berth,' the man replied, without hesitation.

Well, I thought, I can understand that. And why he'd liked to keep certain things secret from the rest of the family.

'James is telling me about the name Young. I feel this name has a connection to his sister.'

'It's his sister's married name.'

'He's telling me that he's met people in the spirit world by the name of Young as well. He's telling me that since he's been in the spirit world he feels like a different character. More patient, more mellow.'

'Well, that's good news.' The man in the audience chuckled. James had wanted me to pass on that he knew he had been withdrawn and almost mysterious when he was alive in the physical world, and was almost apologizing for his standoffish manner. He was taking this opportunity to reconnect with his family and tell them he wanted to be part of their lives again, even though he was in spirit. It's a message that's commonly relayed by those in spirit to their loved ones: that they're still part of their lives.

Gathering evidential information from those in spirit can be a huge way to convince those alive in the physical world that their loved ones can still be part of their lives. I was in Bournemouth at a public demonstration when I connected with two men: Cyril and Arthur. I was relaying this to a man in the audience, who was saying he knew them and that they were brothers – his grandfather and great-uncle. The two men started to tell me what they had done when they were alive in the physical world: they were both army men. The man in the audience chuckled and said it ran in the family – he was in the army too. As soon as he acknowledged the information I was giving him, the men in spirit started to show me numbers. They came in a rapid sequence, so I relayed them as quickly as I could. After hearing them, the man in the audience was speechless. Eventually he told me this was his own army serial number. When the audience heard him say that they gasped. This was highly evidential information, which only that man could know. Not even his immediate family or close friends would have known the number. But there were Cyril and Arthur, relaying very specific information from the spirit world. They also wanted to let the man in the audience know that they were still around him and part of his life.

The value of that kind of reassurance cannot be underestimated. It helps to ease grief and to let people know that the role played by their loved ones in life can continue in spirit. And the evidential information? That's the great proof. If someone hears their loved one in spirit pass on information only he or she can know, it shows them that there is life after life.

My time on the road has been full of such stories. Some are amazing, others sad; a few are even funny. But they're always full of specific personal information. That's what I pride myself on.

But, as I've said, life on the road is far from glamorous.

I get booked for all kinds of events in all parts of the country – at spiritualist churches, in hotels for conventions, and theatres. If I'm to make a theatre appearance, I might have a dressing room to relax and meditate in, which is always a real luxury. But sometimes, just sometimes, I have to make do with the conditions I'm given, and they're not always conducive to relaxing and meditating.

As you know by now, meditating is key to how I prepare before I give a reading, whether it be private or public. As I've mentioned, I always like to take half an hour or so to tap into the energy around me, put out some intentions and ask my guides to help me make as strong a connection to the spirit world as I can. That's the perfect set-up, but sometimes life on the road is less than perfect.

I once did a public event in Portsmouth at a hotel-cum-pub. It was a psychic supper, which was held in a function room upstairs. At the bottom of the stairs there was a kitchen, and the main bar was at the front. You'd think in a hotel there would be an empty room where I could gather my thoughts for a short time before demonstrating, but no. The only relatively quiet place in that hotel was the stairs: I had to sit down and meditate on a step. People were arriving for the event and walking past me, nipping out for a cigarette and pushing by, while kitchen staff with plates, both full and empty, squeezed through. It was a challenge, but there was nothing much I could do about it. Luckily I knew my meditation by heart and could block out any noise or interruption. If I hadn't been able to link up I wouldn't have been able to do the event and would have looked like a failure, unable to help anyone. I managed to get my head straight just in time and the evening went well, but it would have been good to have a little quiet space.

But be careful what you wish for. That's another thing I've learnt along the way. I once did a demonstration in

Kent and had to link up in a storage cupboard! The demo was in a community hall, and all the rooms were in use because a small psychic fair would take place later in the day. At the back of the hall I managed to find a storage cupboard – full of stacked-up chairs and tables – with just enough space for me to sit on a chair. When it came time for me to do my thing, I popped out of the cupboard, which took everyone by surprise. 'Boo! Here I am!'

I once made an appearance at a bowling club in Southampton, which was hilarious for lots of reasons. There was just one big hall, no spare room in which I could link up. The only place where I might get a bit of peace and quiet was the staircase (again!) behind the hastily erected stage at the back of the room. There was only one problem: the stairs led up to a snooker room. As I was centring myself I could hear muffled chat coming from behind the door, and as I was silently meditating, a chap in his late fifties walked up the stairs to go into the snooker room. He saw me and said: 'You don't want to go down there, mate.' I asked why. 'They're dealing with the devil.' I didn't have the heart to tell him that I was the main dealer!

It's one thing coping with things when you get to an event, but getting there can also involve the odd scrape. I was to appear at an event in Wiltshire, and drove up with my girlfriend and a few friends for support. I had received directions that the building was behind a police station in a small town. We got to the area and couldn't find the community hall where I was supposed to be, but we saw a police station and a road behind it. I jogged down the road to see if I could find the place. All I came up with were some garages. At the time I had dyed blond hair with purple streaks in it, so I certainly stood out from the crowd.

Just as I was on my way back to the car – which was in the car park of the church opposite the police station – a police car braked hard as it drove past me, dramatically changed direction and sped towards me. A policeman rolled down the window and asked what I was doing. I told him I was looking for a community hall where I would be hosting an event. Before I knew it he was out of the car and telling me I was being arrested on suspicion of terrorism. He took me into the police station and searched me. He wanted to know why I hadn't any ID on me. Once again, I told him I had popped out of the car, where my friends were, to look down that road for the community hall. But he wasn't buying it.

He went off to run a background check on the computer and, to my astonishment, he came back and told me that he couldn't find any Ross Bartlett in Southampton. 'Do I look like your typical terrorist?' I asked, by this stage starting to get a little bit frustrated. 'I'm wearing a suit and a pink shirt! Do you think I'm James Bond or something? Do you think my mobile's going to turn into a grenade? Listen, if you don't believe me, go and talk to my friends. They're outside waiting for me in a silver BMW.'

We marched around to the car, and when we got there, my girlfriend thought I'd found a policeman to ask directions! In the end, we managed to convince him that I wasn't a terrorist and made it to the community hall on time.

Funny stories and scrapes aside, when I get to a location and find somewhere to link up, the real business of connecting to the spirit world and helping people starts. My main goal is to follow Cliff's teachings, and that means getting as much evidential information as I can and conveying it to people in a way that gives them comfort and lets them know that their loved ones who have passed are okay.

I'm lucky that when I make a connection to the spirit world it's so strong and clear that I can bring forward this kind of information. It's extremely rare for a medium to relay evidential details early in a reading, if any at all. Usually there are lots of questions and no real statements. But that is what I do.

Plenty of mediums also like to pass on advice – take this job, don't move house, don't cross the road on Tuesday at 11.07 a.m. – but my mediumship is geared towards proving that there's something else after we pass, that our loved ones live on in spirit and that we're all part of one big energy and consciousness. It's why relaying evidential information is so important: it proves straight away that there's life after death. In fact, evidential information proves that there is no real death, just a continuation. This is what comforts the people to whom I give readings. They hear the information I'm getting from the spirit world, and the knowledge that their loved ones are safe and still part of their lives is all they need to soothe them in their grief. Evidence and information are the key, and the style of readings I give helps to lift a weight off their shoulders.

The evidence comes through in all sorts of ways.

At a public reading in Wolverhampton, I'd managed to get the family name White from a woman in the spirit world – she also passed on that she had lived on White Lane – but her first name wasn't coming through. As soon as a man in the audience confirmed that she was his godmother, the woman in spirit almost instantly showed me an image of a rose, as if she was saying, 'Yes, I was his godmother and this is my name.' I asked her if the image had anything to do with her name. She said yes. The man in the audience was staggered that I relayed her name almost immediately, and comforted that she could communicate and lived on in spirit.

Symbols, images and suggestions all play a huge part in providing evidential information, and as a medium, I've learnt that there's significance in everything that is shown to me, whether it feels relevant at the time or not. Sometimes the information comes in an instant, like switching on a radio, but sometimes I have to work harder and be more aware of the things that are shown to me.

At a spiritualist church in Southampton, I had contacted a woman's grandmother in spirit. The subject was sitting next to a memorial plaque with the names of past church members inscribed on it, and as I was scanning the room, as you do when you're thinking hard about something, I suddenly felt I should take a closer look at the board. I wasn't sure why. But I was being drawn to the board and one of the names … West. Instead of ignoring it, I felt this name had some significance, so I asked if she could understand the name West. West Court turned out to be the name of the block of flats her grandmother had lived in.

Names, surnames, characteristics, town names, a road name, even house numbers … Sometimes even more is possible if the connection is strong. I always try to pass on this information because even the most crowded public reading can turn into an intense, emotional and powerfully healing experience for the people involved when they hear evidential detail.

One of my proudest and most detailed evidential readings was with William and Gladys (you can see a clip of it on my website). I was in a local spiritualist church, and I was communicating with a man in spirit called William. He directed me to a woman in the audience he wanted to talk to. I had managed to determine his name right from the start, and when I asked her if she could understand the name William, she said yes.

'Thank you, William. Do you have anyone else with you today?'

I had a feeling that a woman had stepped forward, and almost immediately William said clearly that her name was Gladys.

'Interesting,' I said. 'William is showing me a woman called Gladys, who has also stepped forward. Can you understand the name Gladys?'

'Yes. William was my grandfather and Gladys was his sister.'

The connection with William and Gladys was clear and strong, and I was being given lots of images and names, all of which seemed important to William.

'I'm getting through a name … Bellemore. Can you understand Bellemore?'

'Yes,' answered the woman in the audience. 'That was the name of the road I used to live on when my grandfather died.'

Now I understood why William was so keen to bring Gladys forward – the road name his granddaughter lived on also had a strong connection to his sister. But he hadn't finished. A sudden flash of numbers entered my mind.

'Can you understand the number one hundred?'

'That was the number of the house I lived in on Bellemore Road!'

There were gasps from the audience.

'I'm getting more numbers. And some letters, too.' I started to reel off what I thought were just random numbers and letters but, as I've learnt, I never discount anything from the spirit world even though it might seem random, jumbled or irrelevant.

'S ... O ... 1 ... 5 ... 7 ... Q ... X,' I said slowly, as each symbol entered my mind. 'Can you understand that sequence?'

'Hmm, I'm not sure.' The woman frowned.

The symbols came through again. The second time I saw them, something clicked: they could only mean one thing.

'Okay, but William seems very insistent on relaying this information to you. Would you understand this to be a postcode?'

'I'm not sure, I honestly can't remember. I'll have to check.'

After the reading she came up to me and explained that she had asked her friend with a smartphone to check the postcode on Google maps: SO15 7QX was the postcode of 100 Bellemore Road. She was flabbergasted and couldn't thank me enough for bringing through her grandfather, who, she explained, had been like a father to her.

During the rest of the reading William had had other things to say. He showed me memory links to his granddaughter's childhood, and told her he knew she had been thinking about her future recently. This woman, William had told me, had a job working with people, caring for them, and in the near future she was going to branch out more in her field. She was to look out for new opportunities, be aware of new things happening and have an open mind when it came to change. William also told his granddaughter that he was looking out for her teenage daughter – giving her energy, making sure she was safe and well – because she had a lot going on at school. It was a crucial time for her, and exams were looming.

After I had relayed this information, the woman was extremely happy. To know that her grandfather was not only alive in spirit but sending her and her daughter messages of love, support and energy was more than she could have hoped for.

Family connections are extremely important and a lot of the time I'm shown memory links by those in spirit. When I link in with a spirit I connect to them telepathically – I feel what they feel and see what they see – and often they will be full of images and feelings from the subject's past. I remember visiting a spiritualist church in Birmingham and coming to two women who were sitting next to each other on the front row. I asked if they were connected in any way, and they explained that they were the best of friends.

To their surprise, I told them that I had people coming through for them both at the same time. I was getting a man called Robert – this was almost the first thing I said to one woman. No flannel, no avoiding the subject – a name, straight away. Robert was explaining that he had passed because of a respiratory condition, and that his illness had been long and painful. The woman on the left understood and confirmed that this was her father. He then showed me a connection to living out in the country, and she said that in his generation they had had a big family who lived out in the country.

But something was bugging me. I had in my mind a reminder of a message I had given to someone else a month or so before. It was a connection to Westfield Road.

'Can you understand a Westfield Road?' I asked her.

After a pause she said, 'I don't think so. That doesn't mean anything to me.'

I went back to Robert, who kept repeating 'west, west, west'.

'Okay, what about the word "west"? It's being repeated to me, so there must be some significance in it. I'm being told that the word "west" is the thing I need to pay attention to. Can you understand the word "west"?'

'Yes!' She almost laughed with relief and surprise. 'West is our family name!'

'I'm getting through that he was quite a strict gentleman but in a nice way. He was very proud,' I said, after picking up more information. I turned my head to the side, took a swig of water and whispered away to Robert.

'He's telling me that there's a lady here too, but she's not coming forward. I do hear the name Shepherd. Can you understand the name Shepherd?'

'It's my aunt's married name,' she said.

'Hmm.' I paused for clarification from Robert. 'Your aunt was a West before she got married, then became Mrs Shepherd. I can feel that now, and she's stepping forward. She's beginning to send feelings about what her personality was like. She feels like a strong lady, very outgoing. A strong character.'

'Oh, yes, she certainly was.' The women giggled.

'Now I'm hearing the name Osbourne. Can you understand that?'

'It's my niece's married name.'

'Your aunt is telling me about the Osbourne side of the family, and that it has been going through difficult times lately. That's what the spirit world has been talking about, and that's why they wanted to come through today. A number of people from your niece's partner's side of the family have been watching over your family recently.'

The women nodded and smiled at each other. I had given three surnames from different branches of the first woman's family, and also memory links from her childhood – images of her activities and the street she'd lived on. Not only that, but because her family had been going through a tough time, she was comforted to know that her family in spirit were looking out for her.

I came to the second woman. A man had stepped forward and told me his name was David. 'Can you understand the name David?' I asked.

'Yes, I can!' she exclaimed. 'He was my son-in-law.'

David began to tell me his story. He had passed very recently and suddenly of a heart-attack and was very young. He said that some of the family were blaming themselves and felt guilty that they didn't know anything was wrong with him and couldn't help him. He wanted to let his mother-in-law know that there was nothing she could've done and he was the only one to blame.

As the woman processed David's messages, more information came through: that his passing was still an emotional subject for the family; that members of his family had been thinking of him, even discussing him on the morning of the reading. He wanted to say to the woman in the audience that he knew they were still remembering him, still loving him. And that feeling was mutual: he wanted to send his love to his partner and their daughter. He missed them all and loved them, even in spirit. And, most importantly, he wanted to alleviate their guilt. The woman was over the moon with this information. She told me it made perfect sense, especially because her family had been talking about David only today, and that she felt so much better now that she had heard what he'd had to say. She rushed home to tell the rest of the family.

The raw emotion that's unleashed when I'm in touch with a family member who has passed into spirit can sometimes be overwhelming. Often the loss of a loved one, especially if that loved one has been part of someone's life for a very long time, leaves a huge hole in their lives. They miss them so much, and often find it difficult to see a future without them. I've been there with Nain and Cliff, so I know how devastating physical death can be to those who are left behind. I want to make the best connection possible for these people to prove to them that their loved ones are still part of their world and always will be.

A private reading was one of the most emotional I've ever had the privilege to give. A woman in her late forties came to see me, and as I showed her into the room where I give private readings, I had a funny feeling that this one was going to be intense. I couldn't put my finger on why. My client was a little pensive, and sadness was etched on her face. She was friendly, but looked as though she might shed a tear over any evidential information I was able to give her. Of course, at that stage I didn't know her story or who I was going to bring forward, so I had the familiar sense of anticipation. The woman, I was sure, had a very definite idea of who she wanted me to bring through for her.

We took our seats, exchanged pleasantries and I began to breathe deeply, tapping into the energy around me and focusing my mind on any spirits stepping forward. Soon enough, I felt a presence. It was the woman's grandmother, but she wasn't there to pass on any information: she had stepped forward because she wanted to bring someone else through. Someone younger. It turned out to be the woman's daughter.

It often happens that a person who has passed away recently will step forward with the help of a relative who has been on the other side for longer. The 'older' spirit will be more accustomed to communicating telepathically in the spirit world and working with energy. He or she will help the 'younger' spirit to communicate, especially if the younger one lacks energy, as tends to be the case with spirits that have not long passed. In this case a great-grandmother had brought through her great-granddaughter.

The girl's mother was in tears as I described her daughter's personality and how she had passed. It had been in a car accident, the mum told me, and she had passed very quickly.

'Is there anything you'd like to say to your mum?' I asked the girl in spirit.

I saw images of a jumper and felt that she was trying to tell me something about it. Feelings started to come through that it was special.

'Your daughter is showing me an item of clothing. It feels important to both you and her. Do you keep this top close to you, perhaps as a reminder? A physical item of clothing that makes you feel close to your daughter?'

'Yes,' she said tearfully. 'I know it's silly but having that top with me just makes me feel closer to her, as if she's still somehow with me.'

As soon as she said this, I felt her daughter smile. I know, she told me.

'Your daughter wants to tell you that she knows you do this. She's smiling about it.'

The daughter showed me images of her bedroom. The bed was made, everything in place. There were photographs on the wall, make-up bags on the dressing-table, CDs and other belongings throughout the room. She passed on feelings that this was how her room looked now.

'Your daughter is showing me her bedroom. Nothing looks out of place. She's telling me that you haven't changed it since she passed.'

'That's true. I just can't. My husband thinks I'm mad, but it was her room and I want it to feel as though she's still there.'

'I understand. And so does your daughter. She's telling me so. She's sad that you're sad, but she understands. And you're right: she wants to let you know that she's still around you. She's still with you.'

At this the mum cried. Sad tears that were also of relief and joy. To know that her daughter was still around her in spirit and aware of everything that was happening in the family home made her smile for the first time. But there was more.

'Your daughter is telling me that …' I focused hard. 'She's telling me there was a present. A present you were going to give her on the day of the crash.'

'That's right. It wasn't a particularly special day – I just saw something in a shop that reminded me of her, so I bought it for her. I never got the chance to give it to her.'

'She wants to thank you. It was a very sweet thought, and she's really sorry you didn't get the chance to give it to her. She wants you to know that she'll always be with you and will always love you. You were always doing things like that for her, and she was always very grateful.'

At this the mother broke down. It was all true, she said. Through her tears, she told me her daughter had died in her late twenties. It must have been heartbreaking that she had lost her so young. But the daughter wanted to pass on one last message: her mum wasn't to feel guilty that she hadn't been there when she died. It's every parent's nightmare to experience the death of a child, but not to be there at the end cuts to the very essence of parenthood – protecting their child. But here was the daughter, telling her mum that it wasn't her fault. Her physical death had been instant, and she was okay. Really she was.

I watched the mother leave the house, shut the door and breathed a huge sigh of relief. Life can be so unfair sometimes, and I was happy, in the middle of all that emotion, that I'd been able to pass on some evidential information. I was also happy that I had put the woman in touch with her daughter again, however fleetingly.

Just as I was going to get myself a bottle of water and unwind, there was a knock on the door. The woman's husband was standing outside. As soon as he saw me he embraced me. 'Thank you so much,' he cried. 'I don't have any experience of this sort of stuff, but whatever you did was amazing and the things you said . . . Well, my wife told me a few of them and they make perfect sense.'

In another emotional reading for a parent a young man stepped forward. He turned out to be my client's son. I established pretty quickly that he had been in the army and, once again, that he had died young. I was getting lots of information through – the names of uncles, grandparents, other relatives – but he seemed stuck on his own name. His mother had confirmed all the information I had given to her, but she was desperate to hear his name. I carried on talking to him, trying to put him at ease, relax him and make sure he was confident enough to build up his energy to the point at which he could give me his name. For ten minutes we talked about how he had passed; it had been very quick, a huge shock. The mother nodded: she told me that her son had died in Afghanistan very recently after trying to defuse a roadside bomb. He had been blown up and wouldn't have felt a thing.

He talked about the family members who were on the other side with him and gave the names of some people he had grown up with who had passed and with whom he was in contact. He talked about his mother and her life and asked me to tell her that certain things were going on in her house, which were signs from him: he had been trying to let her know that he was around.

'He's also asking me to see if you remember him visiting you in a dream recently,' I asked the mother.

'Yes,' she said, surprised. 'He was so clear and vivid it was almost as if he was still alive.'

I immediately started to get other feelings and images – flashes of light, things not working properly. 'Do you understand lights going on and off randomly and electrical items acting a bit funny inside the house? Like they're working fine one minute and not the next?'

'Only last night the light in my hallway was flickering on and off. I thought it was the bulb on the way out, but after a bit of flickering it just stayed on.'

I was getting validation of everything this man was showing me, but he seemed extra keen to let me know he'd been trying to get in touch with his mum. Their bond was obviously very strong, and I sensed his frustration that he couldn't be as expressive as he wanted to be. He kept showing me images of his mum with her back to him, or his mum sitting on the sofa watching television. I knew he wanted to reach out and touch her, to physically contact her, to do the things he had done in the physical world. But he couldn't.

'He's showing me that he's desperate to contact you, to let you know he's around and all right. Can you understand that?'

'Yes,' she replied quietly, staring into the middle distance. 'I sometimes sense someone watching me. It's such a strong feeling. I see something out of the corner of my eye, but when I turn around quickly to see who's there, the presence is gone.'

I asked the young man in my mind if this was how he was trying to communicate with her. He said yes. But still there was no name. Even though I felt the young man's energy was strong, I needed help. I put out a question to Alex: could he show me a picture of someone I knew who had the same name? I needed help from my spirit guides, and Alex was the one I thought of first. Sure enough, an image of a guy I'd gone to primary school with popped into my head. I hadn't seen him since I was ten, so I certainly wasn't expecting the image Alex put through. My classmate's name was Nick. 'Can you understand the name Nick or Nicky?'

'Yes!' she cried. 'His name was Nicholas, but people knew him as Nick or Nicky!'

She went on to explain that she herself had been in the army, and it had been extremely difficult to separate the emotion she felt at losing a child from the objective understanding of a military person that this could happen at any time when you were out in the field. That I'd managed to communicate his name made all the difference to her. From the information he was sharing, she knew who he was, but a name always brings relief and closure to someone who's wanting to get in touch with a loved one, which is why I always try to go in first with a name and build up from there. But sometimes, as now, the name can be hard to hear or see, and that's when my spirit guides and associated images come in handy.

But the reason he wanted to come through and make contact with his mother was simple: he wanted her to know he was all right, always around her and in the spirit world. His passing had been quick and painless, and he would always be there. Always.

Words, feelings and messages from the spirit world can have a tremendous effect on those who hear them. It is incredible to witness the transformation of someone who comes to a reading consumed by grief, nerves and raw emotion and leaves comforted. But contacting the spirit world can also be a redemptive experience for those seeking guidance in their lives.

Two or three years ago a man came to hear me give a reading in a spiritualist church in Southampton. Afterwards we got talking. Before that night, he told me, he had been very sceptical when it came to the existence of a spirit world and mediumship in general. But the reading I gave him was so accurate it had got him thinking. We stayed in touch after the demonstration and he updated me on his exploits: he went to more spiritualist churches and began to explore spirituality and the possibility of an afterlife. He's now president of a spiritualist church in Southampton. His experiences opened a door for him, and his journey – from non-believer to high-ranking member of the local spiritualist movement – has been remarkable.

Another local reading helped to transform someone's life. Last year I did half a dozen for recovering drug addicts at a local halfway house rehabilitation clinic;

it supports people in the second or final phase of their recovery. One of the clinic's employees had seen me host a demonstration, and asked afterwards if I would come to give readings to some patients. It might help them to focus on and develop their spiritual side, which, in turn, might help with their recovery. It seemed a great idea, and when Josef, a young Eastern European, walked in, I knew it was a worthwhile exercise.

In his early twenties, Josef was pale and skinny with a slightly oily pallor. He hadn't taken any drugs for a while, and as he shuffled in, he told me that he was in the second stage of his recovery, but had a long way to go.

'I was curious,' he told me. 'I want to see what this is all about. It's not every day you get the chance to have a reading with a medium. So here I am. Let's see what happens.'

He was right. We had no idea who we were going to bring through, but I liked his openness and, of course, I was full of admiration for his courage in fighting his demons. I hoped I could help him.

First I brought through an old lady, whose name, she told me, was Petra. She was lively and very friendly, and when Josef heard the name and personality traits, he smiled widely. 'That's my grandmother. Her name is Petra,' he exclaimed.

'Petra's passing on lots of love for you, but she's also bringing through someone else. I can sense a man stepping forward. He feels friendly, but stern. Quite a strait-laced gentleman.'

'I recognize him too,' Josef said.

'He's giving his name as Arthur or Artur.'

'Artur, yes. He's my grandfather.'

I brought through both of Josef's grandfathers and he was overjoyed. He had obviously been close to both men, and as the reading continued, the first grandfather told me he had been a major in the military. We went on to share a few memory links and personality traits, but Josef's grandfather wanted to get a few things off his chest.

'Your grandfather wants to tell you something, Josef,' I said.

'Okay, I want to hear it. I miss his voice, but this is fine.' He smiled.

'Your grandfather, Artur, is asking me to tell you that your grandmother and he both know what has happened to you and that you shouldn't blame yourself. We all make mistakes in life. You're no different from anyone else. Life was bad to you and you dealt with it the only way you could. But that part of your life is over now. Your grandmother and he would like you to look forward, and you should know that they're behind you all the way. With you all the way. Stick with it, Josef. Stick with it and see it through.'

Hearing the words and feelings of his grandparents seemed to have a huge impact on Josef. He had been relaxed and amiable when he walked into the reading, but now he gulped back the tears and stared into the middle distance, nodding. But Artur wanted to continue: 'We know you have an interest in bricklaying. You can get a qualification in that, we know you can. Go for it, pursue your dream. Life doesn't have to be like this for you. You can do whatever you want to do. Life is short. Make the most of it,' he said.

And with that Josef was nodding more enthusiastically, acknowledging his grandfather's words with determination and strength. His grandparents eventually said goodbye, and Josef told me he hadn't believed in any afterlife until now: he had been so wrapped up in his troubles that the idea had never crossed his mind. The reading, he said, had made him feel that there was a lot more out there than he had realized. The knowledge that his grandparents were looking out for him, and giving him the confidence to do what he had always wanted to do, was heartening at this stage in his recovery. And to hear that they were giving him energy and strength to combat the darker moments that would come on his journey to getting clean was a big boost. He left me, saying, 'I've got something to live for.'

Some months later I heard that Josef was doing fine and that he had started a course to gain a qualification in bricklaying and building. His grandparents had helped in spirit. Josef had had to find the spark within to help himself.

The Missing Woman

As I've mentioned before, I just don't know who I'm going to be communicating with at any given event. I can't plan – I may begin with a reading that is highly disturbing, then give another, just minutes later, that is funny and heartwarming.

I was at a public demonstration when a man stepped forward in spirit. He informed me that he had passed in a motorcycle accident, and pointed me towards a man in the audience. When I asked the audience member whether he could understand the man in spirit who had passed in such an accident, he told me he knew of two people who had passed in that way. I needed to narrow it down. I managed to get a name.

'Can you understand the name Darryl?'

Astonished, he said: 'Yes! My name's Darryl! But I knew someone who died in a motor accident called Darryl too.'

I was starting to get more information through. The Darryl in spirit was telling me that he was in his mid-thirties when he passed, and that in the physical world he had been a bit of a joker and lived his life as if he didn't much care what anyone thought of him.

The Darryl in front of me chuckled and nodded in acknowledgement, accepting the information I was giving him. But then something extraordinary happened. While I was relaying Darryl's information, an image flashed into my mind of him dropping his trousers and mooning at me, then at the audience! I had never seen anything like it in a reading before. Audience member Darryl had told me that his friend had been a joker, but to this extent? It was a formal gathering with people clutching handkerchiefs and tissues in case they got a connection to someone who had recently passed. I wondered if they were ready for such a lighthearted image. I took a deep breath and told Darryl what his friend in spirit had done. He laughed, as did the whole spiritualist church.

'That definitely sounds like Darryl!'

The risqué image didn't just make people laugh: it acted as a key piece of evidential information to describe Darryl's personality. He sounded like a brilliant fun guy.

As I mentioned earlier, a demonstration at a public event may start off with one type of reading but subsequent readings change the mood. I was at a demonstration in the south-west of England and had linked up with two men. They were steering me towards a woman, so I asked if I could talk to her. Surprised and a little nervous, she said yes. That's the standard response from anyone I go to during a public event – who could it be? What are they going to say? Everyone's going to be looking at me!

I brought through the first man, who was giving his name as Charlie. I asked her whether she could understand that name. She frowned and looked quizzical for a moment, trying to remember if she'd known a Charlie among her family or friends. Suddenly her face sprang to life. 'Yes,' she said. 'Charlie was my uncle.'

But then I felt another presence. Another man had stepped forward, also giving his name as Charlie. I was scratching my head, asking myself what the odds were against two people with the same name coming through.

'Another gentleman has stepped forward, and he's also giving his name as Charlie. Is that something you can understand?'

'Yes.' She chuckled warmly. 'Charlie was his dad, my great-uncle.'

'Well, I have both of them here waiting to talk to you!'

She was speechless. She managed to muster a 'Wow' and an excited gasp as she turned to her friends. While she was getting used to the idea of two spirit relatives coming through, I was busy trying to decipher what they were talking about. They were like-father-like-son, two peas from the same pod, and good fun. They told me that when they were alive in the physical world they hadn't believed you could make contact with the spirit world – it was impossible. I was passing all this on, as well as describing their very dry sense of humour, and the woman in the audience was laughing and agreeing with the personality traits I outlined to her. After they had sent their best wishes to their niece and great-niece they left, chuckling as they stepped out of my focus. It was another nice reading, full of fun and fond memories, and that I had linked up with two people from the same family, with the same name, made it one I would remember. The next reading – the last of the evening – I would also remember, but for different reasons.

I went to a man at the back of the audience and asked if I could talk to him. When he'd agreed, I got to work, trying to figure out who from his family had stepped forward.

'You're not going to believe this,' I said, 'but I have two gentlemen here who are giving me the same name. Jack. Their names are Jack.'

This had to be some sort of record: two readings in one night, with two pairs of men who had the same name. Two Charlies and two Jacks. I couldn't believe it!

'Yes.' He chuckled. 'They're my uncle and great-uncle.'

Again! This was definitely something interesting. Two readings, two sets of uncle and great-uncle with the same name. I was shaking my head and smiling – what are the odds? – when I started to centre on another man who had stepped forward.

'Another man is here,' I said. 'He's giving me the name Jim.'

'Jim was my grandfather.'

'Thank you,' I said. 'One Jack seems to be the person who is speaking the most. Let me see ...'

Jack, the uncle, was difficult to understand – he was throwing images, feelings and thoughts at me but they were jumbled up. Everything in his communication was a muddle. During most readings I receive images, feelings or voices in a linear fashion, but with Jack it was like hearing poor reception on a radio. I couldn't understand what he was trying to say. It felt important, so I wanted to get the information right, whatever it was. I had to concentrate very hard, because the connection was unusual: Jim, the grandfather, wasn't saying anything, but he intimated to me that he had stepped forward to give energy to help Jack become the main communicator. Now yet another family member was stepping forward, this time a woman called Caroline – but she was silent too. It seemed that almost an entire family in spirit had stepped forward to make sure this message got through loud and clear. Sometimes during readings a spirit will appear to help boost the energy and strengthen a connection of someone else, rather like one of my guides.

'Can you give me a minute?' I asked. 'I'm trying to unravel what your uncle Jack is telling me.'

I turned my head slightly to the right and began to whisper my questions to Jack. He was passing on feelings that I was still struggling to understand. There was sorrow. There was emptiness. There was a void. They were feelings that, thankfully, had been rare in the readings I had given before, but here they were, bringing almost a crushing sense of sadness. As I've mentioned before, I just don't know who I'm going to get through and what kind of information I'll be asked to pass on. The majority of spirits I link with give names, family details, memories, road names and other specific, evidential information. But this was different.

The sadness and emptiness he was conveying were such desperate, strong feelings I could only think they were being felt for someone else: the kind of sadness you feel for someone close to you if something awful has happened to them; the kind of gaping chasm in someone's heart when a loved one goes through a horrendous ordeal, when you know they're suffering and there isn't anything you can do to help. It felt as if something had happened to someone Jack cared about. Something awful. The more I channelled these feelings the more I felt strongly that something had happened to a member of Jack's family. Was it someone in spirit who hadn't yet stepped forward, or someone in the physical world? Perhaps it was the man in the audience.

It was tough because I was aware that this might be sensitive information and a roomful of people was waiting for an answer. I had to play this the right way in case unpleasant information came through. And then I got a little clarity from Jack. The feelings suddenly became stronger and clearer. Jack seemed to indicate that someone in his family had gone missing, and that now this person was in spirit.

'Can you understand anything about someone in the family who has gone missing? I'm getting a strong feeling from your uncle Jack that there's someone like this in the family,' I said.

'Yes,' he replied quietly, after a pause. 'My aunt went missing some years ago and we haven't seen her since. We didn't know whether she was alive and just missing, or whether she had died.'

I nodded, but already I was getting more information. I saw a shoe in my mind lying in undergrowth. With all the other things I had felt – and information that the aunt was missing – the image was chilling, showing me the aunt had been taken from us. I kept feeling the sadness, the overwhelming helplessness, so I decided to end the reading and speak to the man privately afterwards. From what I had seen and felt, it was obvious what had happened to this woman.

'Well, your uncle, great-uncle and grandfather are telling me that she is all right,' I said to the man in the audience. 'She's in the spirit world and she's being protected. I don't know whether you knew she was in spirit, but that's what I felt. Your relatives told me they're with her and looking after her. They want you to know that.' I added that I would like to talk to him in private and pass on the information I had gleaned from her relatives in spirit, which I didn't feel comfortable revealing in front of a large crowd. I serve the people and the spirit world, not myself. And I remembered this when I realized what they were telling me. I could have passed on the information in public, but it would have been a sensationalist's way of doing things. I'm not in this work for the shock value or making myself look good. Some information is just too sensitive to reveal in a large crowd. It wouldn't have been fair on the man in the audience. I'm even uncomfortable writing about it here, in the most public way possible, but I want to illustrate that a medium's job and the readings he or she gives can range from the happy and emotional to the sad, horrid and emotional.

I told the man about the shoe I had seen in my mind, and he explained that when his aunt had gone missing ten or so years before, the family had never found out what had happened to her. As sensitively as I could, I said that I was getting strong feelings from his relatives that his aunt's life had been taken from her. I apologized for the upsetting nature of the information, but I felt it was my duty to tell him everything I had received. He nodded and thanked me, telling me that this was the first time anything like this had happened since his aunt had disappeared and that, ever since, her family had been looking for answers. What I had told him didn't seem to have upset him. It was more of a relief, he explained. To hear that his aunt was in the spirit world, being looked after by her family, had been comforting.

We said goodbye and I, too, felt relieved – you never know how a person is going to react after hearing information of this kind (how would I feel?). I was also happy that I'd done the right thing in saying these upsetting things to him away from the public forum in which all eyes would have been on him.

Later that night, on the drive back to Southampton, there was silence in the car. We had all been part of an amazing evening, with readings revealing polar opposite types of evidential information. I thought deeply about the man, his aunt and the lovely family who were taking care of her in the spirit world. It was one thing giving readings and passing on information: I had got used to that and I was good at it. I had reached the stage where I didn't give it a second thought. But this? For the first time in years I'd felt pressure. Pressure to get the information absolutely right. I couldn't afford to make any mistakes, especially if I was going to receive more upsetting information, as I had that evening. I had to dedicate myself to finding ways of strengthening my bond with the spirit world. I had to be prepared for anything.

Keith's Story

I certainly wasn't prepared for what happened a few months later. I was in a car full of friends, driving along the south coast. It was dusk and we were not far from Wymering Manor – it was reputed to be haunted, but I had never visited. It turned out that one of my friends in the car – who had managed mediums before and is gifted herself – knew the owner, so she suggested popping in to say hello and see who we could find in the spirit world. I don't do this very often, but I was with friends who were all in the industry, so it seemed like an interesting idea.

Wymering is the oldest building in Portsmouth, first recorded in 1042 and mentioned in the Domesday Book. Once owned by King Edward the Confessor, it passed into the hands of William the Conqueror after the Battle of Hastings. To say it has history is an understatement, and it's reputed to be one of the most haunted houses in the country. TV shows have visited it and ghost hunters have tried to see the spirits reported to wander its corridors. A little look round told us that this was a special place – it still looked quite grand even though it had fallen into disrepair – so we sat down to see what or whom we could contact.

There was a table in the room, so we decided to use table-tilting as a means of bringing through any spirits that were in the area. Mediums commonly use the technique to ask the spirit world to contact the physical world – it's as simple as it sounds – but I'm not altogether keen on it. It's a bit showy. But there we were, and my friends were egging me on to use the table. It was getting late and I was tired, but I centred and focused myself and, as we were sitting around the table, I asked the spirit world to make themselves known to us and tilt or move the table, if they could, to confirm their presence and signify that they wanted to communicate. Sure enough, as I was putting out some intentions the table started to move. One friend said she could feel the presence of a child, and a very specific child. Inwardly I groaned because I had felt the same presence, but everything that I was getting from it was . . . Well, let me continue the story.

Once we had made contact we couldn't stop there, although I could see where it was heading from pretty early on in the reading. We asked the child to move the table to the right to answer yes. The table moved to the right. The spirit had definitely stepped forward. There was no going back now. We asked the child if he or she wanted to communicate and, again, the table moved to the right.

How old are you? we asked the spirit in our thoughts. Are you between nought and ten? Move the table to the right for yes, to the left for no. It moved to the left. How about between ten and twenty? The table moved to the right. Using the same processes, we managed to decipher the spirit's actual age and sex: a boy of twelve. My friend whispered that she knew a boy who had passed at twelve. We needed more answers.

My friend asked if he was connected to anyone around the table. Again, the table moved to the right. Yes, he was. My friend looked shocked. Is your name Keith? she asked. The table moved to the right.

Would you like to speak through one of the mediums here? Again, the table moved to the right. Who would you like to speak to? We all spoke our names, and he soon gave us his answer: that little boy wanted to speak directly to a medium and, you guessed it, he chose me.

Even though I was wary and wanted a night off, I started to communicate. By this stage I had moved away from the table and was sitting on a step in the freezing cold. There was no heating at Wymering. I didn't want to be there or give this reading, but I could see in my friend's eyes that it meant a lot to her, so I had no option but to continue.

'Well, Keith, it's nice to meet you. Thank you for stepping forward. What would you like to tell us?'

I heard a little giggle in my mind.

'Look, here's me glasses!'

I saw a pair of old-fashioned spectacles and a flash of blond hair in my mind.

'Thank you, Keith.'

My friend knew who Keith was, but I still didn't.
For the most part it was just another reading, but there
was something different about it. I felt the innocence of
childhood, but also the desperation of someone who had
experienced something horrific. Keith went on to tell me
some of the most shocking things I've ever heard. By now
he was in full flow, wanting to talk, wanting to show me
more of his everyday experiences as a little boy. Running,
giggling, playing in the street. Normal things. Judging by
some of the images he was showing me he wasn't from
our time. There was something about the nature of his
clothes and his local surroundings – knitted waistcoat,
short trousers and cobbled streets – that suggested
he had lived in the physical world in the middle of the
twentieth century. Despite the innocence of these
images, sadness lurked in the background, informing
everything. I wasn't sure I wanted to see what had caused
it but my friend was almost shaking with anticipation.
I was getting hideous feelings.

Almost immediately my hunch was proved correct:
Keith began to show me what had happened to him and
how cruelly he had been treated. I was shocked beyond
words. It came through in images, feelings, sounds and
voices. As we were communicating, he was back in that
awful place and I began to see what he was seeing. He
was showing me because he wanted me to know. He was
showing me because he wanted other people to know.

A flash. An image. Walking. A suburban area.

A feeling. Warm skies, dusk. A feeling. Fear. Then horror.

An image. A van. A rope.

An image. A cigarette burn. Tears.

A voice: 'Aw, you want your mam, do you?'

A feeling. Horror. Fear. Desperation. Alone. So alone.

A feeling. Being hit hard. An image. A bruise. A cut. Blood.

A voice through gritted teeth: 'You still want your mam?'

A feeling. Hot breath on skin. Pain. Tears. Tears.

An image. A plastic bag. A piece of string. Hands around the neck.

A feeling. Can't breathe. Fear. Fear. Fear. Then quiet. Wind blowing. Then quiet.

An image. A cross.

A voice. Cross. Cross. Cross.

I gulped hard and held my head in my hands. I had never seen or felt such things. As I was relaying Keith's graphic retelling of what had obviously been the last moments of his young life, my friend had her hand on my shoulder, confirming everything that I was saying.

Then Keith, as calm and relaxed as you like, said: 'There's more stuff. More stuff I want to tell you. Next time. I'll tell you next time. I have to go now.'

And with that he was gone.

In the car on the way home we were quiet. I was mentally and emotionally exhausted. I was huddled in the back seat because it had been so cold but also because I felt like protecting myself against the images and stories Keith had shared with me. His own story.

I think it's important to share with you Keith's shocking story just as my friend did with me on that fateful drive home. Where to start? My friend told me his name was Keith Bennett and he was taken from his family, aged twelve, in 1964 by two people: Ian Brady and Myra Hindley. On that warm summer's evening he was on his way to his grandmother's house near Manchester to meet the rest of his family when Brady and Hindley approached him in their Mini pick-up van and asked him for help with loading some boxes. What's a little boy of twelve going to say to a request like that? Brady and Hindley drove him out to Saddleworth Moor, where Brady, carrying a spade, walked with Keith onto the moor telling him they were going to look for a lost glove while Hindley stayed behind to keep watch. Brady returned some thirty minutes later without Keith. He had, he told Hindley, sexually assaulted the shortsighted child, who had broken his spectacles the day before, and strangled him with a piece of string, burying him on the moor.

His resting place has never been found, and his mother Winnie campaigned tirelessly to find her son ever afterwards. Keith was the third of Brady and Hindley's five victims; all were under eighteen, four were sexually assaulted and all were murdered between 1963 and 1965 in and around Manchester. Keith was taken just four days after his twelfth birthday.

My friend explained that she was a close friend of Winnie and had played an active role in the search for Keith's body.

It's a matter of public record that Brady had taken a photograph of Keith before he buried him, and Winnie – quite naturally – never asked to see that horrifying image, even though it had been in police hands ever since Brady and Hindley were arrested and their home was searched. No one else has seen that image, yet I was able to describe some of Keith's treatment, injuries and feelings. It didn't make me particularly proud, and even though it almost brought me to tears, it was information I had to relay. My friend, who has been party to information that either hasn't been released to the public or is not widely known, confirmed everything I had passed on.

It was a night I would never forget and, as my friend was telling me Keith Bennett's story, I realized the full significance of what had just happened. I hadn't asked for it. I'd wanted a night off. But I can't choose who I bring through, and it seemed that Keith was desperate to tell someone what had happened to him. It may seem strange that he came through in a location on the south coast, when he'd lived up near Manchester, but there are no geographical restrictions in the spirit world. It doesn't matter where I am, or where a spirit lived in the physical world: if they come through, they come through. That was only the beginning of the story, though.

Some weeks later, my friend called to ask if I could do a proper reading and contact Keith again. She was intrigued by his last statement: 'There's more stuff. More stuff I want to tell you. Next time. I'll tell you next time.' She wanted to know more, not least because she was involved in trying to help Winnie find Keith's body. I wasn't sure it was something I wanted to get into, especially after the images he had shared with me the last time we had communicated.

'Ross,' she said, 'I've been to plenty of mediums in the past and you're the only one I truly believe has a gift. The others I've seen have either got something through, then lost it, or have been faking. You're the only one I trust. Even if we get nothing, it's worth a go.'

So, tentatively, I agreed. After all Keith had 'chosen' me to speak to and my friend was desperate for more information. So I went to her house, where she had set up a video camera to record everything, and got to work. I wanted it to be over as quickly as possible. I could just see the headline, 'Wacko psychic contacts Keith Bennett!' and I didn't want that to happen. My friend and Winnie had had so many crackpots and fakes down the years, claiming they knew where Keith is buried or what really happened to him. And I know that many people reading this will scoff and say I'm just telling the story to make a name for myself – they definitely will after what I'm about to tell you.

After my routine I was as relaxed as I could be, given the circumstances, and ready to begin. I sent my intentions and prayers to the spirit world and my guides, asking them to help bring Keith forward. And, almost immediately, he was there.

'Hello again,' he said, quite cheerily.

'Hello, Keith. Thank you for stepping forward. You mentioned last time that you had more things to tell me.'

'There are others like me,' he said. 'Others like me up on that moor. No one knows about them, but I do. They're there, just like me. A lot more children went missing. They haven't been found, but they're there all right.'

'Thank you, Keith. You say there are more like you, but a lot of people want to know where you are on the moor. Can you help us with that?'

'Cross,' he said. 'Cross.' And then he showed me an image, like 'X marks the spot' on a map.

'Cross, Keith? Can you explain the cross?'

There was silence. I really hoped I hadn't lost contact with him because he'd seemed so eager to talk and our connection had been so strong.

'Keith, are you there?'

More silence.

'Keith?'

An image of a woman with a stern face and a shock of blonde hair entered my mind. There was a coldness about her, a feeling of isolation, of pain and rage. I knew instantly who it was. There was no mistaking it.

It was Myra Hindley. The woman who, with her partner Ian Brady, had murdered five children in the 1960s and had been one of the most reviled women of the twentieth century. Books had been written about her; television programmes and films had been made documenting her life and the terrible crimes she had committed. Even to this day, there's a fascination with the Moors murders and their perpetrators, which means that whenever there's a story about Myra Hindley it's guaranteed to make the front pages, even though she passed in 2002. There had been a lot of news recently, for instance, involving Ian Brady, and Winnie's fight to find out the burial place of her son, so I do not tell this story lightly. I'm fully aware of the sensitivity of the case, the grim fascination with it and the outrage a lot of people still feel when they think about Hindley and Brady. Once again, I tell it because I feel I have to, not to seek publicity or cause a sensation, but because Keith chose me to convey some of the information regarding his life and to illustrate how unpredictable and tough a medium's work can be.

'I'm Myra,' the woman said.

I didn't know what to say. What can you say to a woman who lured five children to their deaths? What

can you say to a woman who was complicit in some
of the cruellest and most graphic crimes committed
in the twentieth century? What can you say to a woman
who is still regarded with so much hate and revulsion?
I shivered and my skin crawled, but I needed to find
out why she was there. There had to be a reason. There
always is.

I cleared my dry throat and composed myself. 'Thank
you for stepping forward, Myra,' I said, taking another
gulp between sentences. 'What would you like to tell me?'

'I know what you think of me,' she said, the feeling of
coldness and detachment now very strong in my mind.
'I was mentally ill, I know that now. When I passed I
was in such a dark place. I didn't know what to think.
I had been waiting for that moment ever since ... those
horrible days. But when I got here I was confused, upset.
Didn't know where I was. Some people I met here helped
me, reassured me that I was all right. I feel much better
now, and I'm trying to do whatever I can to make up for
what I did.'

She still felt stern and cold as she said this. I was not
there to pass judgement or offer her forgiveness – that
was the last thing I could ever do. I was there simply to
pass on information, for Keith's sake.

'Myra, can you give me any more information about
the case? Information I wouldn't know?'

Even though I knew who Keith Bennett was and who
Ian Brady and Myra Hindley were, my knowledge of the

actual case was sketchy to say the least. An image of a gun entered my mind, as well as images of burnt photographs in a basement.

'We had a gun,' she said. 'They have it now. They have everything. They have the photographs. They have the gun.'

My friend nodded. Yes, she said, the police still have the gun and some photographs that have never been seen or released to the public.

'I am so sorry for what I did. Can you tell Winnie that? Please, can you tell her that? I will never forget what I did, ever. I regret everything.'

'Okay, Myra,' I interjected, almost not wanting to hear her pleas. 'When we spoke to Keith before, he talked about a cross. Can you help with that? Can you tell us what it means?'

'Adam,' she replied. And there it was again. The image of a cross in my mind. It was constant. Cross. Cross. Cross. It was extremely significant.

'Adam,' she said again. 'Adam.'

The image of the cross, then the name Adam. And then Myra Hindley was gone. Keith stepped forward in her place and again he was most insistent.

'Adam. Cross. X marks the spot,' he said to me. 'Adam. Cross.'

I looked to my friend, who was nodding quickly and writing everything down. She whispered that, yes, there was an area called Adam's Cross on the moor, and that other people had wanted to search there. It was the part of the moor that was mentioned most often in connection with Keith, but we had just got some evidential proof of it from Keith himself and the woman who had lured him to his death.

'Adam. Cross,' he said again. 'Adam. Cross.'

And then he was gone. The little boy who had stepped forward on a night when I would rather have been at home had bravely revealed the answer to a mystery that had been perplexing police and family for more than forty years. But pass on a message of sorrow to Winnie? From Myra Hindley? That was something I just couldn't get my head around. How do you say to someone who has lost their son in the most cruel and public way that the woman who was central to this act of barbarity wishes it to be known that she's sorry? I feel uncomfortable to be telling you this story, and I can only imagine how Winnie felt when mediums like me turned up on her doorstep to tell her they had been in touch not only with Keith but also with Myra Hindley. It must drag up all kinds of emotions.

All I can tell you is what came through from Keith and Hindley. I didn't choose for them to step forward, but they obviously had information they needed to give me. And despite the continuing uncertainty as to the whereabouts of Keith's remains, I truly hope that, with her recent passing, Winnie will now have found some degree of peace.

Keith was aware that people were still looking for him, so it was important for him to convey this information. I don't want to be insensitive and I don't want to provoke outrage. I just want to help people and, in Keith's case, I hope that in some small way I have.

The Lakota

The need for knowledge and
learning was never more urgent. Life on the road had
taken me to all kinds of places, and I'd met so many
different people in the physical and spirit worlds. One
thing was clear: I had to be prepared for anything and
everything, which meant improving my technique and
my connection to the spirit world. Especially if I got
involved with someone like Keith Bennett again. People
would demand facts. Pure, evidential information was
needed more than ever so I needed an even stronger
connection with the spirit world. It was time to seek
fresh sources of knowledge and new techniques,
wherever they came from.

When an Internet DJ friend of mine suggested I get
in touch with medicine men from a Native American
tribe, I jumped at the idea. We had just finished an
interview for an online radio station when she told me
she knew someone in her native country and would
put me in touch with him. As you know, when I was in
my early teens, school had held no interest for me, but
now that I was gaining momentum as a spirit medium
I wanted to gobble up all the knowledge I could find.

After I'd first spoken to Mountain Horn I'd become fascinated by ancient cultures, and was drawn to the way in which Native Americans used mediumship as one element of a complete healing service. Wherever you look in ancient culture – whether Native American, Aboriginal, South American or African – a medium was so much more than we consider them in today's Western society. A medicine man or shaman was the bedrock of any community, providing mediumship, healing and counselling. You consulted them about a wide range of ailments, both physical and mental, and they set out, with the spirit world, to solve the problems of their fellows. It was the same for the Lakota. An offshoot of the Sioux, their reservations are in South Dakota, the state slap-bang in the middle of America and near to the border with Nebraska.

My DJ friend said she would put me in touch with a Lakota medicine man, if I was interested in finding out how other cultures accessed the spirit world. She runs a spiritualist centre in New Jersey and I was welcome to come along and have a look at it any time, she said. She would introduce me to some of her Native American friends.

I didn't need to be asked twice. I felt I could learn something from these people that would help me in my quest for better connections with the spirit world.

I was eighteen when my girlfriend and I visited New Jersey. We were met at the airport by a friend of my DJ contact, and in no time we were on our way to Chicago to meet the medicine man. Soon I was shaking hands with a middle-aged man. He wore simple clothes – baggy black trousers and a black shirt – but he had an air of calm and authority. If you saw him on the street you wouldn't give him a second glance, but as I listened to him speak there was something about him that intrigued me. He was a man of few words, but every now and then he said something that made me chuckle. I knew within ten minutes of meeting him that we would get on well.

During our first conversation he asked about what I did, then explained his role in his community. He told me stories, and I was enraptured by his voice. Sometimes I found him a bit hard to understand, mostly because of his terminology, but his tales were full of wonder. The only other times I've listened to stories and been transported to another world was when Nain sat with me at bedtime and told me about her childhood in Wales. The medicine man told me about his tribe, his ways and his beliefs in regard to the spirit world. I had to listen carefully because he asked me questions about what he had just said. I learnt very quickly that the Lakota like to keep secret the names and precise details of their rituals (I haven't named my medicine-man friend out of respect), because over the centuries much of what the Lakota hold dear has been ripped away from them. It's heartbreaking but, like many poverty-stricken communities, their fierce spirit and generosity survive unquenched.

Later on the medicine man encouraged me to give him and some of his friends a reading. The Lakota don't have mediums as such in their culture: everything is much more intertwined with the spirit world. A medicine man is in charge of communicating with spirits but also offers guidance to people with other problems, physical or spiritual. My new friend was curious to see how I worked. The man he asked me to read for was called Shaun, and I was already anticipating a challenge: cross-cultural readings are always more difficult, not because the connection is weak but because of the kinds of information that come through. Would I be able to understand names, places and pieces of information specific to the Lakota culture? There was only one way to find out.

As we sat down I was aware that two people had stepped forward. The first was an older woman, who was showing me an image of holding a baby. The links I was making with her were giving me the feeling that she was a grandmother, and that the baby signified a loss. The loss of a baby in the family. I could feel what she was feeling, and she was showing me the baby to pass that message to Shaun.

'That makes sense.' He nodded. 'My family did lose a child.'

I registered a man stepping forward. He showed me an image of a horse. As I was focused on it, I realized through his feelings that this wasn't anything to do with owning a horse: the animal was being shown to me to signify a name.

'I'm being shown a horse,' I told Shaun. 'But it isn't any horse in particular. I feel really strongly that the horse is part of this man's name.'

'Yes. The last part of my grandfather's surname was "Horse".'

It's not uncommon for Native Americans – male and female – to have names dedicated to animals. Sitting Bull. Crazy Horse. Black Elk. Shaun's grandfather had had a similar name. Memory links I was tapping into showed me a dirt track that led to a house, which had a garden with a big tree. Shaun's grandfather showed me the young Shaun climbing the tree, eager to get as high as he could. Shaun laughed and said he used to do that at his grandfather's house: he'd climb as high as he could, then look out across the Lakota reservation and gather his thoughts.

The reading wasn't finished yet: the grandmother stepped forward again and showed me a feather. It felt as though it had extreme significance, and when I mentioned it to Shaun, he nodded.

'Whenever a Lakota graduates from high school he's presented with a feather. It's tradition,' he explained. 'And when I graduated my grandmother came with me and she gave me the feather. It's such an important thing for any Lakota to receive that feather, and when I think of my grandmother I always remember it. We were close.'

His grandmother was making the point that she remembered the significance of handing over the feather as clearly as Shaun did, and that she still holds that proud memory. The bond was still there between them. It would never be lost.

As the reading came to a close, Shaun and the medicine man seemed pleasantly surprised. Although they were deeply spiritual people and, they had told me, were used to contact with the spirit world, they had never seen a medium from my culture give a reading like that. We shared some common beliefs, just practised them in a different way.

Now I had to return to New Jersey for the next leg of my trip. I'd arranged to teach a number of workshops at a spiritual centre there. My medicine-man friend would fly down a few days later and I was, I learnt, to be taken to a special place to learn more about the Lakota and some of their rituals. I couldn't wait.

When the medicine man arrived, we drove to a house outside town where those interested in Native Americans and their rituals could sample their way of life. But before I could learn more, I was asked to do another reading, this time to a man called Michael. He lived on the Lakota reservation in South Dakota but was visiting New Jersey and was intrigued by my way of connecting to the spirit world.

As I centred myself and linked up, a man stepped forward. He told me he was Michael's grandfather and showed me that he had passed after a stroke or a brain haemorrhage. When I relayed this information to Michael he told me he didn't know of anyone who had passed in that way. I scratched my head. The man who had stepped forward was insistent that that was why he had passed into spirit and wouldn't take no for an answer.

'I'm sure he didn't die of a brain haemorrhage,' Michael said. 'My grandfather was in the hospital for liver disease. That was how he died.'

He told me that his grandfather had passed when he himself was very young, but he could remember spending time with him and having a really strong bond with him. But he had no memory of a brain injury. I went back to the grandfather to ask him if he could be clearer, but he replied with the same information. Michael frowned again so I asked him to talk to his family. Perhaps the information from his grandfather had been jumbled.

I had to carry on. More information came through. There were details about this man in spirit's personality (bold, upstanding, strong, quite a big build), which Michael understood, and about Michael's son, who, the man in spirit said, he was looking out for and would always be around. He talked about a car Michael once owned and how he had tried to catch his attention by turning on the windscreen wipers randomly. Michael laughed: it turned out that so many weird things had happened inside that car that his friends had nicknamed it the 'ghost car'. Then I got a name, spoken to me very clearly.

'Can you understand the name Bobby?' I asked.

'Yes, that was his name. It's definitely my grandfather.'

'I'm also getting images and feelings that show me he worked with horses out in the country. Can you understand that?'

'That was what he did for a living. He bred horses on the reservation.'

I had established a great deal about his grandfather, but the manner in which he had passed was still a sticking point. The grandfather was telling me one thing, but Michael was insisting it had been another. Once again I asked him to talk to his relatives, to satisfy my own curiosity as much as anything. Like my medicine man friend and Shaun in Chicago, he had approached the reading with a mixture of intrigue and caution, but left impressed and happy. I had helped him to communicate with his grandfather as well as showing him the way I contact the spirit world. In giving him a reading I felt as though I had participated in a true exchange of cultures and ideas.

Now I was to experience one of the Lakota tribe's key rituals: the sweat lodge, or the purification lodge. Native Americans go to a sweat lodge to pray to the Great Spirit and the rocks used to heat the place, which are sacred to them. In Europe, the closest we have to a sweat lodge in physical terms is the Scandinavian sauna, but the Native American equivalent is far more intense. Rocks are heated in a fire and taken into a small, tent-like structure and placed in a pit in the middle. The structure is tiny – about half the size of a normal bedroom – and sometimes the entire tribe has to fit into it. There, in the stifling heat and packed together like sardines, they will offer prayers, cleanse themselves and focus their minds on their ancestors and the Great Spirit.

It was a warm late afternoon when I reached the house in New Jersey. The Lakotas, including my new medicine-man friend, teased me about how hot it would be, but I was looking forward to it. How hot can it be? I wondered. I stripped down to my shorts and took in a towel with me. Tradition dictates that the men go into the lodge first, so there was no ducking out now – I was one of the first in. That was fine by me: I was up for the challenge and eager to experience what the Lakota did regularly. I was hoping for a pure, spiritual experience, and to find a stronger, even more meaningful way to connect to the spirit world. The entrance to the lodge was minute, so I had to crawl through the flap, then pick a spot and sit down cross-legged.

The glowing rocks had been in a fire for some minutes. When they were brought in I could feel the heat immediately – and I wasn't ready for it. It was so hot in there it hurt to breathe. I watched the medicine man sprinkled cedar shavings on the rocks, and as they caught the heat they started to sparkle, a magical sight.

The heat was making me prickle all over and I was sweating like crazy. People were sitting right up against me. There was no room to move. It was overwhelming. Twenty or so people, jammed into a tiny space with intense heat, took some getting used to. Then a few men, the medicine man among them, starting chanting, saying prayers and pouring water onto the hot rocks. Hissing steam filled the structure, and the very dry heat quickly became wet and heavy. It clung to the walls and formed into droplets. In no time I was soaked – each time the medicine man sprinkled water on the rocks a new wave of heat engulfed us.

As the steam rose and circulated around the lodge, the chanting swelled. A musty smell flared my nostrils, and as the steam continued to circulate, I struggled to maintain my composure and adapt to the heat. I focused on the hypnotic chanting, which was almost like wailing and felt primordial, ancient. It drew me in until it had locked me into its rhythm. I felt lightheaded. I had never experienced such intensity. You're expected to do four 'rounds' in the lodge in one session, each lasting around twenty minutes, so even though it was pitch black I was aware that people were moving around – some wriggling to get comfortable, others leaving because they needed air. But it didn't matter. The singing, chanting and praying had an unbelievably calming but energizing effect on me. It's difficult to explain, but the constant hum meant I was able to focus on the sounds instead of the heat.

Soon I was getting used to it. It had been tough but my body was finally acclimatizing. Now I was starting to understand what it was really all about. This millennia-old tradition is a cleansing process, a balancing process, and a way to flush the toxins from your body and focus on the thing that matters most: connection with the Great Spirit.

To begin with, my lips felt as if they were burning, my tongue was on fire and my lungs were about to explode. But as time went by I could focus on the chanting and ignore the physical pain. It reminded me of when I was training for martial arts. During those practices I was focusing so much on the moves that any physical pain or tiredness disappeared. It was the same with the sweat lodge.

I completed the four rounds. I learnt how to control my breathing. Not too short, not too deep. Relaxed and rhythmic. If my breaths were too short or too deep, I took in too much heat and my body panicked a little. I had to find a happy medium and focus on the chanting. It was a very good illustration of mind over matter, and by the end of my first sweat lodge I felt uplifted, light as a feather and really energized. It was an incredible sensation.

I had to go back the next day and do it again. Even though it was a form of physical suffering – I was crouched, with people almost literally in my face and that unbelievable heat swirling around me – I could already understand why the ritual had lasted five thousand years.

It was challenging, but it was a great way to shed all that the Western world had stuck to me, and to empty my mind. This was what Cliff had preached in his circle: to tap into that reservoir of energy you must empty your mind completely. I had found it difficult at first, but now I could empty my mind and meditate in the most unusual and noisy places before any public event. If only I had access at those times to a sweat lodge!

After I'd got used to the heat and focused on the chanting, I could empty my mind of all thought more easily than ever, so I needed to step up to the challenge and do it again. I hadn't contacted any spirits in my first sweat lodge, but I had a strong feeling that the more I did it and the more used to it I became, the more things would happen.

In my second sweat lodge, I was packed in right at the back, in the middle of the lodge, the hottest part. I was focusing on the chanting again, drifting and swaying with the sounds. I felt my mind moving with the vibrations. Suddenly a hand touched my back. There was no one behind me and no space for someone to get their hand round, but I felt a hand on my back and then my shoulder. I didn't recoil. Instead I remembered something my medicine-man friend had told me: that often in sweat lodges spirits come close during ceremonies and rituals and might make contact in a physical way. In the Western world, a physical manifestation of a spirit is seen as a rare, headline-grabbing event. But the Lakota consider it perfectly normal. It's just a way in which the physical and spirit world become one; a way to honour and communicate with their ancestors. The spirit who had interacted with me didn't leave a name or a message. It simply touched me. It was so unlike what I was used to when I gave a reading. I was accustomed to spirits stepping forward, having conversations with them and gaining evidential information. This was a pure, raw interaction.

With the chanting and singing, the atmosphere was crackling with an energy I hadn't experienced before. It was as if the medicine man was creating a special ambience so that a spirit could step forward and manifest itself in physical form. His chants seemed to call the spirits. And, for a brief moment, a spirit who had accepted the call had interacted with me. It was amazing.

I was almost at the end of my stay with my DJ friend when I was invited to a sacred ceremony, and was warned that this would be a two-and-a-half-hour stint so I had better get comfortable. It would take place in a tepee, and as we went towards it, in the grounds of the house in New Jersey, my medicine-man friend asked me to sit close to him, near a sacred altar space in the middle of the tent.

Soon after I entered the tepee, the lights went out and we were engulfed in darkness. Drumming started, then chanting and singing. It wasn't long before the atmosphere was crackling. When I focused hard enough

I found myself becoming one with the ceremony. With a tepee full of people doing the same thing, the combined energy was an overwhelming sensory overload.

My medicine-man friend gently touched my hand, and I took hold of his. I did the same with the person sitting on my other side, so that we were linked physically as well as mentally. With each moment the drumming and chanting intensified, and that was when I noticed something above our heads. A green fluorescent light glowed, then flashed on and off. At one moment it was there, at the next it was gone. Then it flashed on again, but this time it started to move around the tepee. It darted off to one part of the tent in time with the drumming, then back into the inner circle where I was privileged to be sitting. At one point it drifted within inches of my face, then sped off. The only time I'd seen something vaguely like this was in Cliff's garage, when we had experimented with the spirit trumpet. But this manifestation of spirit was unlike anything I had ever seen. I say 'spirit' because what else could it have been? Everyone except the drummers was holding hands at that point in the ceremony and there were no lights or light switches. And the ceremony was designed to summon spirits. It seemed that this level of physical activity in spirits was quite usual to the Lakota.

Just as I was trying to get my head around the dancing light, I noticed something else. Native Americans see the rattle as a sacred instrument and use it to summon spirits and for spirits to communicate with the physical world. It's often made from turtle shell or leather, and filled with clay beads or seeds. The rattles used in this ceremony, however, were filled with quartz crystals – and suddenly they sprang into life. But it wasn't any physical person using them – remember, our hands were linked or drumming. Even though it was pitch black the rattles were shaking so hard that the crystals inside were smashing together, which made the rattles glow in the dark.

And what fun the spirits had with them! I heard one high in the air, and then it was much closer, almost level with my head. A moment later the noise was somewhere else. I could hear rattles everywhere, and they were providing a relentless percussion to the drumming and chanting. It was like being in a band – with two members from the physical world and one from the spirit world!

The intensity was building to fever pitch. There was a lot going on in that tepee, but the experiences of physical mediumship were far from over. The rattles themselves were producing little white sparks that flickered up into the green light – I had green light with pure white sparks exploding all around me. I was awestruck and my mouth fell open. And that's when I felt it. A rattle moved closer to me, the percussive shake ever louder. It stopped in front of me. I looked hard into the darkness to try to see it, and it tapped my forehead. Just a light tap. Then it rattled like a snake over my shoulders, from one to the other, and moved away. As I was trying to process this information, it was back like a shot, tapping my left knee, then the right. It moved up to my chest and tapped over my heart. Then it circled my body. Not only that: it brought with it a voice, perhaps a child's. A voice in the open. Not in my head: it was there for everyone to hear. It gave a playful, high-pitched giggle, and as the rattle was circling me, 'he' began to touch me.

What's going on? Who's touching me? What's touching me?

With what felt like little fingers, he touched my face and squeezed my nose, giggled and sped off.

Keep calm, keep calm. It's only a spirit trying to say hello. But I feel so light-headed with the rhythms and the lights and the constant rattling. Breathe deeply; remember the exercises you learnt in Cliff's circle.

It seemed he was playing a game, and he touched me two or three times, giggling all the while and pinching my nose again.

I was reeling. The lights, the rattles, and now a childlike spirit was playing with me. It was an incredible example of physical manifestation. I hadn't seen or felt anything like it before, and I haven't felt anything like it since. I'd heard that Native American culture was fantastic for physical manifestation, that their rituals and ceremonies were geared up to summoning spirits and letting them heal and energize you. But this? It took my breath away.

The same childlike presence appeared the next day. My girlfriend joined me this time, and the ritual took place in a sealed room in the house. Once again the rattles and drumming were going ten-to-the-dozen but this time a voice began to sing along. Even though it was dark, we knew there were no female Lakota in the room, and the doorway had been sealed with duct tape, so no one could get in or out. But there was the voice: female and very definitely Lakota. Once again it wasn't a clairaudient sound – a sound existing beyond the reach of ordinary experience: everyone could hear it. The rattles were in the air again, darting around the room, banging into the walls and sparking on impact.

And there was the presence I had encountered in the tepee – that playful, childlike spirit. Once again he made physical contact with me, this time dancing his fingers all over my body. My girlfriend and I were told that under no circumstances were we to reach out and touch anything because it might frighten the spirits coming through, so I sat there feeling the tickling sensation the spirit was inducing.

And then he spoke to me in my mind in his high-pitched voice.

'Hello, can you hear me, sir?'

'Yes!' I said aloud.

He went to my girlfriend and asked her to put out her hands. When she did so she felt a light contact jump from one hand to the other. My girlfriend was interested in the spirit world but she had never experienced anything like this before. I reassured her that this was the first time for me too!

But that wasn't all that happened. Before the ritual a blanket and some ropes had been placed in the centre of the room, and one of the participants, during prayers, had put out a thought to the Great Spirit: he needed help with his decision to either move house or stay in the same area. When the lights went on at the end of the ceremony, he was wrapped in the blanket and tied up with ropes. He told me afterwards that a child had taken his hand and walked him around the room without touching anybody (remember, it was pitch black), then led him to the altar area where, in a flash, the blanket enveloped him. What an answer he'd had! He was no longer considering the house move.

After the ceremony was over, I stepped outside and let my eyes adjust to the light. My medicine-man friend asked: 'When are you coming back?'

I didn't leave it long. It was May when I first visited the Lakota in New Jersey, and by the end of July I was back with them, this time at their reservation in Pine Ridge, South Dakota. My medicine-man friend had suggested I visit them again to take part in more rituals and observe the Sun Dance ceremony. It was exciting to land in Rapid City, get picked up by his mother and drive to the reservation. As we travelled across the plains the landscape was truly awesome. It took my breath away.

It was just so big. There was desert as far as the eye could see, with huge, gnarled mountains framing it, then beautiful clear blue lakes and big fluffy clouds in a sky wider than I'd ever seen before. Trees, forests, rocks. I felt so small among all that natural beauty, so different from England where everything was tiny in comparison.

This expanse of natural beauty disappeared as we entered Pine Ridge. We drove through the outskirts of the reservation, and the harsh existence of the Lakota became painfully apparent. There were trailer parks and burnt-out houses, while the carcasses of cars and motorbikes were strewn across roads and driveways. It was shocking. The Pine Ridge reservation is the eighth largest in America, with about thirty-eight thousand people living there, but it's also one of the poorest places in the country. You hear that Native American culture in the US has it tough – there are no jobs, no money and alcoholism is rife – and now I could see the poverty for myself. The land of a proud, spiritual people has been taken away from them, their beliefs shunted aside and their very livelihoods destroyed.

I was there for the construction of the Sun Dance site and to take part in the ceremony. To be invited to help with and observe the festival was an honour. The celebration is traditionally Lakota in origin, and signifies life and rebirth. The real action takes place in the late stages. When the sun rises on the fourth day before the end of the festival, an invited guest (only invited guests may attend) will make his or her way to the centre of the Sun Dance site and dance for four days without food or water (a few sips are permitted in the morning and the evening) in time to the rhythms of drums and chants. At the start and end of each day they do a sweat lodge. Even though only Lakota can officially take part in the Sun Dance, observers may join in unofficially. And I wanted to. I hadn't come all that way to stand on the sidelines – I wanted to test myself and experience some of the things the Lakota experienced.

I would dance as much as I could. I knew it was going to be tough, but I was excited. The participants dance non-stop around a tree that has been cut down and positioned upright in the middle of the site, like a huge maypole. I could do my thing in the shelter I had helped to erect, where other interested observers would gather. I wouldn't be in the open like the Lakota, but I intended to match them step for step, if I could.

Dancing without food and water was one thing, but I was looking forward to witnessing other features of the festival. On the third day of the Sun Dance piercing takes place: men and women lie down in a row and little hooks or pegs are attached to their chests. Each hook or peg is tied to a rope, which is connected to the tree. They dance and pull on the ropes until the hooks or pegs snap out, taking with them shreds of skin, which are placed at the foot of the tree as a sacrifice. It sounds a bit brutal, but it's the most sacred part of the ritual and I wasn't about to argue with it.

First I helped to construct the ceremonial site. It was a hot day – nudging thirty degrees – but the sense of excitement and community meant that everyone was in a good mood. I was involved in building the wooden structure we would dance in, hanging painted and camouflaged netting over it and generally making sure it was sound. Each part of the reservation has its own festival ground, and ours was expected to attract more than three hundred local people. People who came to dance erected little tepees outside the main structure to rest in, while others were there to watch and worship in their own way.

The day before the Sun Dance was devoted to the tree. I was part of a fifty-strong force that lifted it from the lorry in which it had been delivered and carried it to the site. People attached ritualistic flags and prayer ties (like I use in my own rituals) to it, making it the centre of the festival and a sacred object.

I had been on the reservation for almost three weeks and each day I would do sweat lodges and prepare myself for the Sun Dance. The sweat lodges on the reservation were even hotter than I had experienced before, but they were also a bit bigger so the heat and steam circulated more evenly. I don't think you ever get used to that heat, but because I was doing them every day I found them less uncomfortable. The lodges teach you how to focus harder and concentrate on the chanting, so as the Sun Dance approached, I felt I was prepared and ready.

It was four o'clock in the morning when I was woken by my medicine-man friend chanting through the reservation's Tannoy system. By the time the other Sun Dancers and I reached the main festival site, it was almost sunrise and time to dance. To be a Sun Dancer you're required to do seven or eight dances throughout the day, each one with four 'rounds' lasting around thirty minutes. They're totally unlike anything Michael Jackson would have done. Instead they're composed of slow movements, almost walking on the spot, moving to the left slowly and deliberately, and raising your hands to the sky when you feel like it. Remember, they have to be performed for four days without food and water, so gently does it.

Day one was progressing nicely. I stuck to the shelter on the side of the great circle where I was shaded from the sun. From that vantage-point, I watched the Sun Dancers in the middle of the circle, learning the importance of certain chants. Some would respond to different words with different movements, and during that first day I watched and learnt until I was confident of getting into the zone and working naturally with the words and the rhythm of the drums.

Day two was harder. Much harder. It started off in much the same as as day one, but as the time wore on, fatigue crept in. I had been on my feet and dancing for most of the day without food and water, and I was starting to feel weak. My movements were slow and laboured.

The heat was becoming unbearable and my feet were going numb. The sun was blazing down, but at least I was under cover in the shelter.

What the hell are you doing this for? When can I have some food? When can I have some water?

As I was asking myself these questions, I realized I didn't have any answers. I fought my physical desires, focused on the movements and chanting and soon the hunger pangs diminished. But my thirst did not. I was parched. I needed water badly. Another person in the shelter was struggling and had become very weak. At the end of that second day he gave up. He was just too thirsty.

Somehow I was still there. That night I took a few sips of water and slept in the tent I had erected beside the circle. As the third day dawned, I staggered back to the shelter. I can't really explain how the mind takes over in situations like that, but by now I almost couldn't feel myself physically. I couldn't feel my legs or body. It was as if I existed in mind only. I kept going – I must keep going – but I was so weak I was almost collapsing.

Focus, focus, focus. This is the only way you're going to get through this. This is the ultimate test. You can do it. You can do it. Mind over matter. Focus on the chants and the drums, focus on your own meditations and focus on the movements of the Sun Dancers circling the tree.

I was putting out as many intentions as possible.

Alex, Red Moon, Mountain Horn, my spirit guides, please hear me. Please give me the strength to get through this experience. Help me to focus my mind, overcome my physical fatigue. Give me all the energy you can.

Day three was the piercing day, and I watched between my rounds as the hooks or pegs were inserted into bodies, then tied to the tree for the dancing and sacrifice of skin. In my exhaustion it was like watching a surreal movie. People giving back a piece of themselves to the Great Spirit, dancing, chanting. I sat down between rounds, too physically knackered to do anything else.

Day three was almost done. As round three of the dancing started, I climbed to my feet and knew I had no energy left. I stumbled to the dancing area and swayed. My head was lolling, my legs were like jelly and my knees almost at the point of collapse. I lifted my hands when the others lifted theirs, and I moved my feet when they moved theirs. I couldn't think, feel or even see properly. Everything was reflex, and all movement made on a subconscious level.

In that state the rhythm of the drums kept me going. With a relentless beat, they propelled me on, guided and gave me strength. Near to the end of that day, I was being carried by the movements of my fellow dancers and by the drums. That was all I had. There was certainly nothing left inside me: I was utterly empty.

And then something extraordinary happened. At my lowest ebb I felt a sudden rush of energy from nowhere. As the drumming continued, I felt as though I was flying away. Suddenly I was dancing harder than I'd danced at any point during the whole festival. It was like being in a trance and I was filled with electric energy.

The ceiling of the shelter felt as if it was getting higher and higher, and then I heard a familiar voice: 'Keep going, Ross,' Nain said. I didn't question it because rational thought had gone and I had entered into a whole new realm of consciousness. Looking back, I would've wondered what Nain was doing in the middle of South Dakota, but her soothing voice gave me fresh impetus.

Then I heard, 'Keep going. I'm always with you. I'll help you when you need it.' This voice was different, unfamiliar. An old spirit with an unusual accent. But he was there and he was telling me that everything was going to be all right. To this day I have no idea who he was, and he hasn't appeared to me since.

I opened my eyes. I looked at the tree in the centre of the dancing area and it was as if I was looking at myself. I felt as though I wasn't just one part of the tree, I was the tree. I was the roots, the branches and the bark. I was the tree and the tree was me.

When the round finished, I sat cross-legged but couldn't keep still. My legs and arms were shaking, my feet still tapping to the beat. I was utterly spent physically, but my mind was still going like the clappers. It was behaving as though it was separate from my body with an energy all of its own, but within thirty minutes I was out like a light, sleeping under the stars.

Compared to day three, day four was fairly easy. Yes, I was exhausted, but I felt mentally fresher and I got through it without the previous day's difficulties. It was as if I had broken through some sort of barrier and, on the other side, I felt much better. Because the end was in sight and the ceremonial grounds were near the middle of the town, I nipped to the shops between rounds to stock up on the food I was going to eat afterwards. I bought peaches, water melon, a big sandwich from Subway and a tub of cookies-and-cream ice cream.

When the dancing finally ended, I collapsed on the ground. I heard my heart thumping in my chest and was elated to know that I had survived. The heat from the last four days had sucked all the energy out of me. I drank water — a lot! — and took part in the feast the community had put on after the festival. Eating, drinking, pausing, then eating and drinking some more. At the end of the day I fell into a deep sleep.

It took me several days to recover from the ordeal of the Sun Dance, but I was so happy to have taken part in it. For the next week or so I had a big smile on my face. I listened to the Lakotas' stories, drove out to the Wounded Knee monument (which commemorates the Lakota massacre by the 7th Cavalry Regiment in 1890), did more sweat lodges and even gave some readings.

There was also an opportunity to say goodbye to Michael, to whom I had given a reading in New Jersey.

I was walking around the reservation one day when a car pulled up. A familiar face popped out of the window.

'Hey, Ross,' he called. 'How you doing? Come over here, I need to talk to you.'

I sidled over to the car. 'Hey, Michael, I'm good, thanks. How are you?'

'Fine. Enjoy the Sun Dance? Hey, listen, you know you gave me that reading? Well, I got back home and asked around. You were right, man. I was always told my grandfather died of liver disease, but when I asked my family they said that wasn't strictly true. He was in the hospital because of liver disease, but he fell out of bed and banged his head. It was the head injury that did for him. Amazing, really.'

Michael's grandfather had known the truth.

At the end of my trip I didn't want to go home. Although they live in poverty, the Lakota were so welcoming, so generous and so spiritual. Different families had put me up during my stay, and I'll always be grateful to them. I left Pine Ridge with mosquito bites all over my body, a stone lighter and with a renewed thirst for knowledge.

I had been privileged to observe and dance at the Lakota's most sacred festival. Not only that, but I had learnt so much about myself along the way. I had discovered how hard I could push myself, how much physical pain I could endure, how strong my mind was and what it would take to become the medium I wanted to be. Lakota rituals are very different from what we're used to in our material Western world: everything is geared to worshipping the natural world and achieving a state in which the physical and spirit worlds mingle and co-exist. So, when I hang my Lakota prayer ties round my neck and under my shirt for every public or private reading I give, I'm doing the same thing: I'm trying to access a place where the physical and spirit worlds meet.

Healing Grief

On my return from the US I felt re-energized by my experiences with the Lakota. It had become clear to me during my time there that much of what the Lakota do – the rituals they perform and the celebrations they take part in – is geared towards healing.

Whenever anyone talks about healing they're usually referring to a wound that's slowly closing. In physical terms we might administer some cream, take a pill or put on a bandage, but for the most part healing happens in accordance with a natural process. It's much the same with emotional or spiritual wounds. My readings can act as the cream or plaster. They won't heal an emotional wound completely, but communicating with a recently lost loved one in spirit can help.

I was in the English Midlands giving a public demonstration and had brought through a woman called Winifred. She had pointed me towards a woman in the audience. I was getting quite strong feelings that Winifred was from an older generation of this particular family, and when I asked the woman if she understood the name Winifred, a very senior member of her family, she said she did, and that Winifred had lived a long time ago.

But Winifred was bringing someone else through. I had the impression that she was stepping forward to help the other person, a man, make a connection. When he finally stepped forward, he said his name was James.

'I know the name James,' the woman in the audience said. 'He was my husband. He died very recently, so I'm still very emotional about the whole thing. As are my family.'

I began to establish personality traits, to share memories and decipher any images that came through. James showed me a very specific image. I saw a woman outside with a transparent urn that contained ashes. She was scattering them. But there was more. James was putting thoughts in my mind that told me that these weren't human but animal ashes.

'Well, it's funny you should tell me that,' the woman said, after I had relayed the information. 'Only this morning I was scattering the dog's ashes in the garden. He was our dog, my husband's and mine, and he went very recently too. You know, it was just something I had to do. He was part of the family and we loved him so much. In fact, I had the urn with my husband's ashes in the garden too, but I decided against scattering them.'

James wanted to tell her two things: that he was still part of her life, and that he was aware of what was happening and what she was going through; but also that their beloved dog was with him in spirit, and he was looking after him.

After the demonstration, I thought back to other readings that had featured animals. Over the years I've brought through dogs, cats, horses, ducks, hamsters, rabbits and even a donkey. Each being – human or animal – has their own unique personality, so it's no surprise to bring through an animal or two during a reading. Many people regard animals as part of the family, and contact with a recently passed pet causes greater emotional impact than anything else I've encountered. The woman in the audience received two reasons to feel better about her recent losses: both her husband and her dog had stepped forward with messages of consolation.

That was an example of a recent loss, but sometimes it's difficult to come to terms with something that happened a long time ago. Time heals, but whenever you're reminded of a loss it hits twice as hard. That's why a connection during a reading can feel like a weight lifted from a subject's shoulders.

My next story comes from Torquay, and is another great example of how a reading can give comfort to someone who has experienced long-term grief. In this instance, the woman in question was dealing with one of the most devastating types of loss: the passing of a child.

I was in a theatre in front of six hundred people, but as soon as two women came through I knew the direction in which I needed to turn. I saw the woman I was looking for and asked her if she would mind me speaking with her. I explained that the two women who had come through were like peas in a pod; they had been very close and had done everything together when they were alive in the physical world. I also picked up the name Rose. The woman nodded, and told me that they were two aunts — sisters — who had been just as I had described. I went on to talk about their personalities, and again the woman was nodding and chuckling. But then the reading changed.

The two sisters told me that they were there to help bring forward another person, and a third female presence stepped forward. I was aware that there was something different about her. She was having difficulty communicating: there were half-formed memories and she lacked personality. Despite this she gave me her name: Lynne.

'Oh …' The woman cleared her throat. 'Lynne was my daughter. Or that was the name I gave to my daughter. I suffered a miscarriage when I was younger and that was what we called the baby. Whenever I think of her, I think of her as Lynne.'

It was an astonishing twist, and a reading that left lots of questions. Can babies who have barely been alive have enough personality to exist in spirit? Yes. Though babies like Lynne never live a full life in the physical world they still have feelings, thoughts and personalities, even if only on the most basic level. And Lynne was proving that point. She was sharing feelings and thoughts with me, wanting to tell her mother that she had been around her and had seen the refurbished kitchen.

The woman in the audience nodded again. She now knew that her unborn baby was safe with her two aunts in spirit.

These stories are surprising to many people, if only because, like animals, unborn babies are the last people they expect to come through. Another story proves a similar point.

I was in the Midlands, again giving a public demonstration to around a hundred people in a spiritualist church. I was aware of a woman called Elizabeth stepping forward, and she was directing me to someone in the audience. As usual I said hello to this woman and asked if I could talk to her.

She recognized Elizabeth immediately, but Elizabeth wasn't the main focus of attention. She was there to help bring through someone called Anne. Thanks to shared feelings and thoughts, I told the woman in the audience I felt strongly that Anne had passed from dementia. I detected a sense of frustration at her condition but also a strong need to be heard.

'Yes, I know Anne,' said the lady. 'But I don't know of an Anne in the spirit world. The only Anne I know is the one I went to visit in hospital this morning. I went to say goodbye. You're right when you say she's got dementia, but she's still hanging on. She's in a coma and doesn't have very long left.'

'So,' I said, needing to clarify things, 'she's still technically alive?'

'Yes. As I say, I went to visit her this morning.'

Incredible, I thought. Here was a woman with one foot in the physical world, and one foot in the spirit world. And she was starting to communicate through me, which told me that Anne was beginning her journey to the spirit world.

Anne asked me to pass on to her friend that she wasn't in any pain, that she knew what was happening and what was going to happen. She also gave me another name: George. The woman in the audience told me that George was Anne's husband. Again, through me, Anne wanted to ask the friend a favour: would she tell George that she was fine and that they would meet again soon? Anne, on her way to the spirit world, wanted to pre-empt George's terrible grief and let him know that even though he was going through a very tough time everything would be all right.

That evening, the woman who had been in the audience sent me a message on Facebook to say that she had passed on the messages to George and already he was feeling a bit better. He was concentrating on making sure he would be strong for his wife as she passed fully into spirit.

Healing can take many forms, and in Anne and George's case it came in a calm-before-the-storm kind of way. And that sometimes happens. People in spirit want to help loved ones in the physical world, even with difficult emotional situations that have yet to take place.

At a public demonstration in Birmingham I was bringing through a man called Edward, who told me to focus on a man in the back row. I told him I had an Edward waiting to talk to him, and asked if he could understand the name. He said yes.

'Edward was the most important person in my life,' he said, 'and my closest friend.'

But I was getting feelings from Edward that seemed to suggest they had been more than friends. Edward was telling me that he was a quiet, reserved man who had liked to keep his cards close to his chest when he was alive. He also said that he and the man in the audience shared many secrets, and even some that their closest friends didn't know about. While the man in the audience didn't completely confirm it, I sensed they had been partners. Much later on, I discovered I had been right.

The reading continued, but Edward wanted me to give his friend a very specific message: that in five or six months' time he would be there for him in his time of need, and that very specific things would be happening to him with which he would need help.

After the reading the man in the audience told me he was a senior member of the church, and that it had been so long since he had received a message that he had begun to think he would never get another! He told me how fantastic it was to receive a message from Edward of all people, his closest and most cherished friend throughout his life. He also said this: 'Everything you told me about Edward was the truth. The truth was there about him.'

We shook hands, then I packed up my things and began the long journey home.

I returned to the church around six months later for another demonstration. As I was setting up, a member told me some bad news: the man to whom I had given a reading last time had passed. Suddenly the message Edward had wanted to convey – that he would be there for his friend when something very specific happened in the near future – made sense. He wanted to be there to help his transition into the spirit world. The two lifelong friends, who had obviously loved each other, were now together in spirit, and I like to think Edward's healing words helped pave the way for his partner.

Secrets and Treasures

'*I honestly don't know* how my grandparents died,' the woman sitting opposite me said. 'I was young when they went. My mum and dad knew, but I was always shielded from the truth.'

'Okay.' I pondered. 'Maybe you could ask some of your family members how they passed, because what they're telling me isn't changing.'

I went back to communicating with the grandparents, who had stepped forward, asking them for some more information.

'I've asked your grandparents if they want to help bring anyone else forward while they're here, and a man called John has stepped forward and wants to say hello.'

'Oh, my,' she said, slightly shocked. 'That's my father. His name was John.'

'Well, he's telling me he wants to say hello and let you know he's still around you, looking out for you.'

'Thank you. That's really nice to hear.'

'But your grandparents are still here. And they want to show me something ...'

The woman had come for a private reading, and as usual I had settled into my routine so I could connect to the spirit world in the strongest way possible. As she had made herself comfortable opposite me, I'd sent out my intentions to my guides and the Great Spirit and relaxed into the right frame of mind. Almost immediately two people stepped forward. I sensed very strongly that they were a male and female presence, and as I relayed this information to my client she edged forward in her seat, eager for more information.

I managed to get more details. The man and woman in spirit told me that they were her grandparents and described how they had passed. The grandmother, she had shown me, had had dementia; her deterioration had been gradual and extremely frustrating for her. The grandfather, on the other hand, had shown me that he had passed of lung cancer.

I relayed this information to the middle-aged woman in front of me and she looked quizzical. It was obvious she had had no idea of how they had passed. But they were keen to show me something. It was a special object that only grandparent and granddaughter would know about.

'I'm getting an image of a ring. It's a gold ring with a ruby in the middle. Is that something you can understand?'

'Hmm.' She paused. 'No, I can't think what that would mean. I don't know of any ruby ring in the family.'

'Your grandmother is really insistent on this one. She's showing me the ring in a way that makes me feel you or a very close relative would have it. Can you understand that?'

'No,' she replied. 'I honestly don't know of any ruby ring in the family.'

The reading continued in much the same way as many others develop: there were memory links, personality descriptions and messages of comfort and reassurance that the woman's deceased loved ones were living on in spirit and playing an active role in her life. But the question of the ring was a sticking point. I wondered as she left whether it would ever be found. It was obviously very important to the grandmother – she seemed to be telling me that this object was a link between her and her granddaughter, something they had exchanged or that had been passed down.

Sure enough, the woman emailed a few days later. First, she thanked me for the reading, and said how comforting it had been to communicate with her grandparents and father. Then, she said, when she'd got home she'd telephoned her mum, asking her to confirm how her grandparents had passed. Her mum told her that the descriptions I had relayed were correct – her grandmother had passed from dementia, while her grandfather had had lung cancer. Then there was the question of the ring. Her mum, the woman said, had been astonished: the grandmother had left the ring for her granddaughter, but the mother had forgotten about it. She apologized and at last gave her her inheritance: a beautiful ruby ring.

Objects owned or used by loved ones when they were alive in the physical world can bring great comfort to those they've left behind. These objects – pieces of jewellery, watches, a pair of glasses, even a walking stick or a teacup – help us to accept that we're still close to a departed loved one. Their significance cannot be underestimated and they often help build links between the spirit and physical worlds.

Recently, a woman came to me for a private reading and I was soon talking with her grandmother in spirit. I brought her through and was relaying as much evidential information as I could: why she had passed, personality traits and memories. Then, suddenly, she showed me a ring: the image of a plain gold band entered my mind.

'Your grandmother is showing me a ring,' I said. 'I feel it's significant because it's being kept in the family still, whereas there's little else of sentimental value remaining. Can you understand that?'

'No,' she answered, after thinking for a few seconds. 'She didn't leave anything to me and I can't remember any members of the family talking about a ring.'

But there was the ring and it wouldn't go away. I asked the grandmother for more information. Could you show me anything else about the ring? I asked. Is it significant to your granddaughter? And if it is, how? Every time I link up with the spirit world I can feel what the person stepping forward can feel, and almost immediately I felt the grandmother was thinking about my client's sister, her other granddaughter.

'You have a sister,' I said. 'The ring has significance for both of you.'

Once again, blank looks. She really didn't know anything about a ring and hadn't heard her sister talk about one. I asked the grandmother some more questions. Could you show me where the ring is? Is it in your granddaughter's house? In answer to my questions, the grandmother showed me an image of a framed photograph of herself. Is this where the ring is? I saw the image again, of the photograph sitting on a shelf, as if to say, 'Look here.'

A few days later the woman emailed, telling me that she had telephoned her sister as soon as she'd got home and asked her about their grandmother's ring. Her sister said she didn't know anything about it, but my client urged her to look for any photograph of their grandmother she had in her house and search around it, behind it, under it … anywhere near by. Her sister said there was a photograph of her grandmother on a shelf in her living room. She put the receiver down and went to have a look. A minute or so later, the woman said, she heard her sister pick up the receiver and excitedly tell her that she had found a plain gold band behind the photograph. Not in a case, just sitting there. Neither woman had had any idea the ring existed or how it had got there. All they knew was that they suddenly felt much closer to their grandmother than they had done for a long time. I like to think the grandmother was smiling widely in the spirit world, knowing that her granddaughters had found the object to which she had directed them.

Detective stories aside, readings can help with much more than physical objects. Simple words that only a person in the physical world and his or her loved one in spirit can know may trigger a rush of emotion and act as proof of a link between this world and the next.

A middle-aged woman came for a private reading recently, and as I was bringing through her mother, it developed into a reading that wasn't out of the ordinary. I had relayed the mother's passing condition (breast cancer) and some of her personality traits (quaint, elegant, gentle), which were all accepted by the woman in my reading room. Her mother was keen to tell her daughter that she was still watching over her and giving her strength when she could.

But then something unusual happened. The mother showed me an image of a camel. It stopped me in my tracks. A camel? Images of animals aren't unusual, but a camel? There had to be a reason for it (there always is) but even though I kept asking the mother for more information, all she showed me was the camel without explanation.

'I know this might seem strange, but your mother is showing me a camel,' I said to the woman.

She laughed, but her eyes welled and a single tear trickled down her right cheek. The camel, although seemingly random, obviously held huge significance to both mother and daughter.

'Before my mum got ill we went on a lovely holiday to Egypt,' she explained. 'We had such a wonderful time, but when we got home she was taken ill and it wasn't long after that she died. She was a big believer in the afterlife, and when she was in hospital she told me that I must go to see a medium and make contact. She promised that if I did that, and a medium was able to bring her through, she would show an image of a camel. It was our little private password, in memory of our holiday to Egypt.'

A few days later she emailed me to thank me. Only she and her mother had known about the camel. Before the reading she hadn't been sure of an afterlife but now she had no doubt that not only was her mother safe and well, but the camel had convinced her that the spirit world existed.

Another reading that illustrated the importance of shared secret words between the two worlds took place at a public demonstration in a spiritualist church in Southampton. I had started to communicate with a man who was pointing me towards another man in the audience. The man in spirit had given me William as his name, so I asked if the man in the audience could understand that name.

'William is my father,' he said.

Again, the reading continued as normal. William was sharing memories of his life with me, which the man in the audience understood, and also wanted me to pass on a message of goodwill to the man's partner, who was sitting next to him.

When they came to chat with me afterwards they were overjoyed, and the man explained that he was a paranormal investigator who had tried and tried again – via various techniques and in different locations – to bring the name William through. He told me that whenever he managed to make contact with his father he had asked him that in future, with a medium, he was to use his middle name as reference, not his first name. That middle name was William, and this was the first time a medium had brought it through. After years of searching, this revelation had convinced him of an afterlife. Who else could know the pact they had made?

These words or objects may be small, but their significance is huge. They can make the difference between someone believing in an afterlife and dismissing the idea that their loved ones live on in spirit. Once that connection is made, however, generations of people are linked.

The Journey Continues

As I finish this book I'm twenty and I know myself better than I've ever known myself before. I know my beliefs and I know where I'm going. I tell myself that this is just the start of my journey, and I truly believe that. Everything I've seen, heard and felt makes me believe more strongly than ever that we're part of one big consciousness, and when we pass from the physical world we enter another realm, another level of energy. And that's what this universe is made up of: energy and consciousness. We're part of one big field of energy. We exist now, and we exist later. We never say goodbye.

In the years since I turned professional, my journey has been incredible. I'm one of the youngest ever professional mediums; the youngest ever professional medium to teach in an official spiritualist church; the youngest ever professional international medium; the youngest ever professional medium to write a book, to my knowledge; and the youngest ever minister of spiritualism. I'm grateful to so many different people that I'm where I am today. As I look at myself, I see Nain and my grandfather, my mum and dad, my brothers, Cliff, my girlfriend, Chris and Gill. I wouldn't be where I am now without them. Even though Nain and Cliff have passed I know they're still with me. I'm grateful to all the people I've met along the way too; the countless people I've given readings to, the spirits who have stepped forward and allowed me to share information with loved ones, and the people who have taught me invaluable lessons.

The journey will most definitely continue. When I first made contact with Mountain Horn, he told me that people in the spirit world were watching my progress with interest. I know this to be true. A year or so ago I gave a reading to a woman in a spiritualist church in Hampshire. I was in full flow, bringing through members of the spirit world for people in the audience, and it was nearly at the end of the event when I felt the presence of a man in my mind. He was showing me a painting of another man whose image I recognized. He looked like Gordon Higginson.

By all accounts Gordon was an incredible medium, and even though he passed in 1993 he's still thought of with much love by his family and many friends, and revered by the spiritualist community. I had read about him as I was growing up and getting into mediumship. He was born in Longton, Stoke-on-Trent, in the early part of the twentieth century. His mother was a medium too, and as I read more about him I realized how much we had in common. He had started sitting in his mother's circle when he was three years old, had publicly demonstrated his mediumship skills at Longton Spiritualist Church on his twelfth birthday and become known as the 'Boy Wonder'. He prided himself on the retrieval of evidential information and the accuracy of the details he could convey, and at twenty-eight he became president of the Longton Spiritualist Church. He went on to become president of the Spiritualists' National Union in 1970 and helped to turn around the organization's fortunes. He served it for twenty-three years and was known as a brilliant teacher, travelling all over Britain to help people. He also taught at the Arthur Findlay School in Essex (it's devoted to mediumship), eventually becoming principal. He had quite a career.

And now here he was, stepping forward in spirit and pointing towards a lady in the audience. As I relayed the information he gave me, she nodded. It turned out she was also a member of the spiritualist community and she and Gordon had been close friends, staying with their respective partners at each other's houses when they were visiting their part of the country. They would stay up late, laugh, chat and eat cake together, and he wanted to let her know that he was still visiting her in spirit.

At the end of the reading there was a message for me, too. He told me he had watched my progress and noted that I was going about things – concentrating on meditation, prayer, learning and gathering evidential information from whoever stepped forward in spirit –

in the right way. He also told me that I would follow in his footsteps and become a leading light in the spiritualist movement, but in my own way. To get such a vindication of my approach to mediumship from someone as important as Gordon was a huge boost. He told me he would always watch out for me.

So, as I look at myself I can see the path I'm travelling along stretching out before me. I've studied elements from different religions and beliefs. From Buddhism and Judaism to Lakota spirituality, and the lessons I have learnt have given me an unshakeable belief that our world can be whatever we want it to be. That the way we perceive things alters the world around us. All realities can exist at the same time. Our very thoughts build our reality. We help create reality by believing. Everything we need to make life what it can be is in our minds, and our minds are our greatest tool in linking up to the world around us, physical or spiritual. Everyone can link up to the spirit world if they want to. It's all around us.

That's why I wanted to write this book – to show that mediumship is not for a few select people. The spirit world is yours as much as mine. Tune your mind into the energy that swirls all around us and you can access the spirit world too. You just have to let go and have patience.

I need to keep learning, keep pushing myself and finding new, better ways to connect to the spirit world. Keep pushing. Keep learning. Eventually, I would like to see the medium's role in the Western world become similar to that of the medicine men and healers of ancient cultures: at the centre of a community providing spiritual guidance.

I do this already to some extent. Whenever I log onto Facebook, I'm inundated with requests to chat. Suddenly I'm negotiating multiple conversations, answering lots of questions. What should I do about my job? What should I do about my relationship? Where is my life going? I don't like giving straight yes-or-no advice. Instead I like to open people's minds to spirituality and ask them to look inside themselves for the answer. I try my best to help, but sometimes it's tiring and I feel the weight of responsibility. But what can I do? My main goal in this life is to help people, and if I want to be regarded in the same way as a medicine man in the Lakota or a healer from an ancient culture, this is the way it has to be.

I find that as the world gets faster and more materialistic, our spiritual side becomes more and more eroded, to the point at which there's nothing left. We're more interested in what brand our next mobile phone will be, how we're going to get drunk on a Friday night or how much money we can earn than we are in spirituality.

I still have a long way to go.

Recently I took a four-day fasting session. It sounds like a strange thing to do, but I need to keep pushing myself, come up with new ways to separate my mind from my body and to improve my connection to the spirit world. I sat in a spirit cabinet – these were first used during Victorian times to hold mediums tightly so they couldn't use any equipment – with a blanket draped over my head and body. I wanted to go without food and water, as I had during the Sun Dance, and to meditate, clear my mind and improve my connection to the spirit world.

But it was cold. There was no heating in the garage I had retreated to, and as evening turned into night and night turned into day, I felt the chill in my bones. Still, I felt spirits swirl around me. There was Cliff, who had stepped forward to let me know he was with me, and Red Moon, who manifested in child form to keep me company. He sat with me throughout the whole experience, not saying a word. His appearance helped and reassured me. And then there was Alex. There's always Alex and, as usual, he was bringing his own special brand of humour to the experience. 'Hmm, food.' He'd chuckle. 'I bet you're hungry, aren't you? Why don't you go and get something to eat?' He was there to help, of course, but he was joking around, like he always does.

By the third day I was tired and bloody hungry. I was freezing cold, too. It was the middle of January and, aside from the odd hoot of an owl, I heard and felt nothing apart from cold. I'd worn two shirts and the blanket over me, but that made no difference. Then Alex's voice called: 'Take them all off. Everything.'

One of the things I've learnt is not to question anything the spirit world tells me. Everything is said for a reason, so before I knew it I was stripping off and sitting down in the cabinet completely naked. Instead of feeling cold, I felt free and uninhibited and, amazingly, I forgot the cold. It sounds crazy, but as soon as my clothes came off I focused harder on my meditations, and the feeling of freedom helped to separate my mind from my body.

So much so that I started to get some very unusual visions. Even though it was pitch black in the garage I looked up and could see a ceiling. It was perfectly illuminated and didn't belong in that garage – it had wooden beams for a start. Then, later in the third day (although it could have been the fourth: figuring out the time was a bit of a problem), I turned to my right and saw a wall with a door. A plain wooden door in a living room. Later, I sensed something to my left, turned my head and saw a wall with a window in it, looking out onto blue sky.

I was trying to process what was going on and what I was seeing, but a spirit I hadn't spoken to before stepped forward and explained that this was my own consciousness travelling into another place. It was my own mind separating from my body to visit somewhere else. It was the first time I had experienced a kind of astral projection. It's something I hope to experience again and hone in the near future.

Everyone was relieved when I emerged from the garage. They had been worried by my latest adventure, but although I was tired and hungry, the experience had been worthwhile. I had once again pushed myself to the point at which my mind had separated from my body.

It's this kind of discipline that I must continue to undertake if I am to become the medium I want to be. I can keep my body pure – I don't eat meat, drink, smoke, take drugs or prescription medicine – but to keep my mind pure and my connection to the spirit world clean and strong, I must keep pushing myself.

I want to experience so much more. I've recently returned from Thailand, where I was able to visit Buddhist temples and learn from that culture. After my time with the Lakota – and my run-in with the spirit trumpet in Cliff's circle – I want to investigate the potential of physical mediumship and explore the phenomenon of spirit manifestation.

I want to make the art of mediumship available to everyone, and I'll give readings to anyone. I'll also take lie-detector tests, because I want people to know there is truth in what I do. I want people to see the universe and the consciousness within it for what it is – all related, all connected. I want to bring through the evidential information that helps people with their grief and proves that their loved ones in spirit are still part of their lives. I want to keep sharing the knowledge and philosophies I discover as I continue my journey. Most of all, I want to help people. That is my path.

Further Information

For more information about Ross Bartlett and his work, please
visit his website at: www.rossbartlettrealmedium.com or link up
with him on Facebook at www.facebook.com/rossbartlettmedium.

Acknowledgements

Thank you to Cliff Haskell and Sue Runcinmen for starting me off on this journey.

Thanks to Paul Hirons for helping me to compile this book.

Thank you to the spirits on the other side that help me with my work. Without you this would have never been possible.

You are never alone.
Your loved ones and the Great Spirit
will be with you always.

An Hachette UK Company
www.hachette.co.uk

First published in Great Britain in 2013 by Godsfield,
a division of Octopus Publishing Group Ltd
Endeavour House
189 Shaftesbury Avenue
London WC2H 8JY
www.octopusbooks.co.uk

ISBN 978-1-84181-422-3

A CIP catalogue record for this book is available from
the British Library.

Printed and bound in Great Britain by CPI Group (UK)
Ltd, Croydon, CR0 4YY

Commissioning Editor Liz Dean.

10 9 8 7 6 5 4 3 2 1